The legend of

ELVIS PRESLEY

For Maxine and Glyn

The legend of
ELVIS PRESLEY

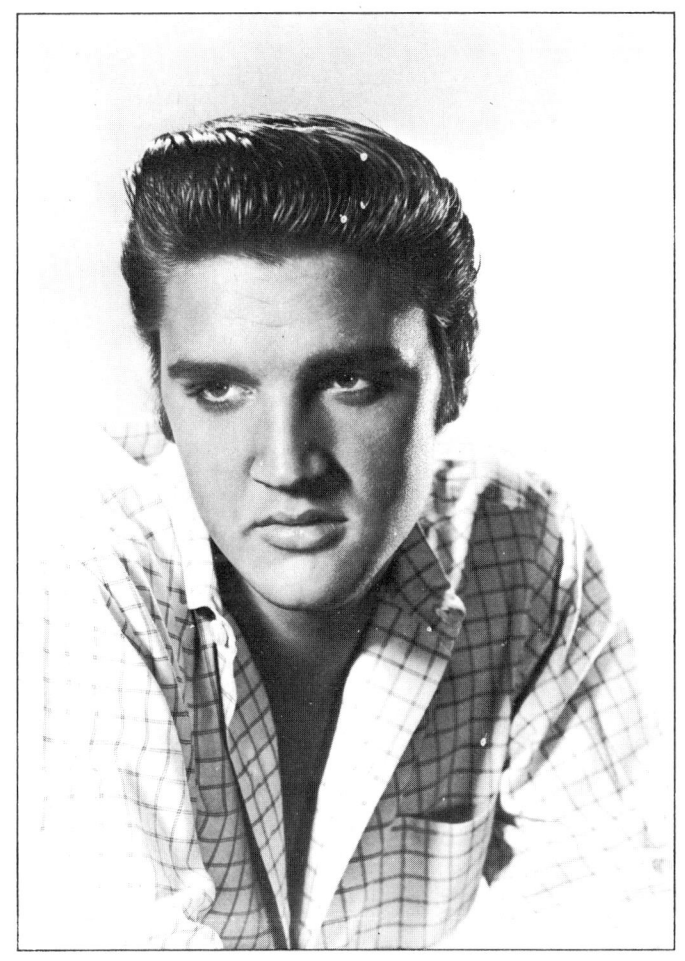

BY W. A. HARBINSON
DESIGNED BY STEPHEN RIDGEWAY

TREASURE PRESS

First published in Great Britain in 1975 by
Michael Joseph Ltd under the title
Elvis Presley: An Illustrated Biography

This revised edition first published in 1977
under the title *The Life and Death of Elvis Presley*

This edition published in 1988 by
Treasure Press
59 Grosvenor Street
London W1

©1975 by W. A. Harbinson

ISBN 1 85051 268 X

Printed in Hungary

The legend of

ELVIS PRESLEY

1

I was a lonely teenage bronckin' buck
With a pink carnation and a pick-up truck.
– American Pie, *Don McLean*

He is born in a two-room plank house in Tupelo, Mississippi. The house is raised off the ground on legs of concrete and brick, has a porch, three windows and a pointed roof. Small, narrow, redolent of poverty, it resists the heavy rains and the summer's dry heat, but otherwise doesn't amount to much. The floors are bare. There is no running water. Outside is a shit-house, a pump, some trees and untended grass. A few miles north-east, in the Princeville Cemetery, his twin brother is buried not forty-eight hours after he is born. Life is raw in Tupelo, Mississippi.

It is January, 1935. Highway 78 runs from Memphis to Alabama, passing close to the Presley home in Tupelo. The land rises and falls, drinks the rain, fights the sun, and is webbed with dried creeks and stooped fences. This is nigger country. There are cottonfields and sugar cane plantations; there is white trash and black scum. You can hear the two groups singing with evangelical fervour in those nights when God keeps them from madness; they both sing the same songs.

About a year after the birth of Elvis Aron Presley and the almost simultaneous death of his brother Jesse Garon, one of history's more catastrophic tornados tears through Tupelo. It spirals blackly to the sky, splitting the dark clouds, ripping through the land with the cold blind malevolence of nature. It's a nightmare, a dreamer's deep trap, the howling eye of oblivion. It kills a few hundred people, injures more than a thousand, and destroys a great number of homes. It takes thirty-two seconds. But the Presley shack, in the east side of Tupelo, remains untouched.

Now we see them. They are a family of three. The mother has

a face of extraordinary beauty, her hair pulled back tight over delicate ears, her eyes dark and luminous. The features are fragile, hinting at deprivation and the sort of religious faith that can move mountains. She is wearing a cheap, patterned dress, a belt buckled at the waist; her left hand is looped over the shoulder of her equally sombre husband. He wears a faded shirt, a hat tipped back on his head; is lean, hungry and radiating the innocence of a man who does not hope for too much.

They are workers and they know it.

9

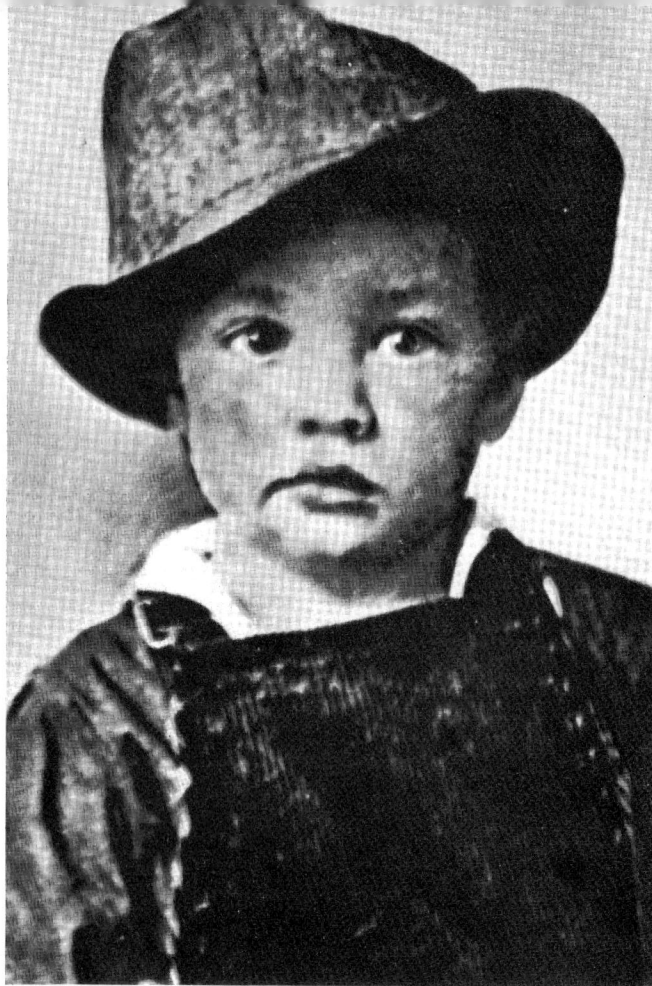

Some time later when the boy is six, there is another photograph. It is a head shot. He has developed some of his mother's more delicate features, is golden-haired, wide-eyed and beautiful. But the famous lip is there, twisted down to the left, giving the angel a mischievous look, again irresistible.

The boy, Elvis Aron, stands between them. He is two or three years old, a real sharecropper's kid. He is wearing dungarees, a grubby two-toned shirt, and has a hat on his head just like Dad. The hat is tipped cutely to the right, slanting down over huge, fine eyes whose pupils seem enormous and give him a penetrating look which is at odds with his round baby face. The nose appears to be flattened, the cheeks are too chubby, and already the now famous curl is distorting his fat lips. He is, in short, an unlovely but irresistible kid – the kind normally doomed to oblivion in a land that eats cheap labour.

When at the age of eight he is photographed again, he is taller, slimmer and quite docile: every mother's dream child.

In this six years the parents have aged considerably. The mother is heavier, her hair is loose but cropped short, and the curve to her legs speaks of hard work. The father wears baggy trousers, a worker's leather jacket and a cheap shirt. The boy, now called Elvis, is dressed in local style, with a long-sleeved white shirt, open at the neck, and ragged trousers tugged chest-high by braces: he is Huckleberry Finn.

The great myths of America lie behind him. Born of a family that is scourged by its own poverty, maybe he already dreams some heady dreams. In this land that he roams, through the cottonfields and swamplands, the air is heavy with the romance of its own history. The Union and Confederate armies have clashed on these slopes, the town has been razed in the fury of civil strife, and the Indians have left names that will roll on the tongue with all the magic of ancient hieroglyphics: this land is a dreamer's masque.

The boy will sense this if he doesn't quite realise it. He will learn to love God, to respect even his worst elders, and to stand by his country right or wrong. He wanders through the bellied fields and the sloping swamplands, puts his ear to the wind and listens closely. The air is filled with singing that came out of slave ships, now pours from black lips, fills white churches. It is the singing of the niggers who have given to the

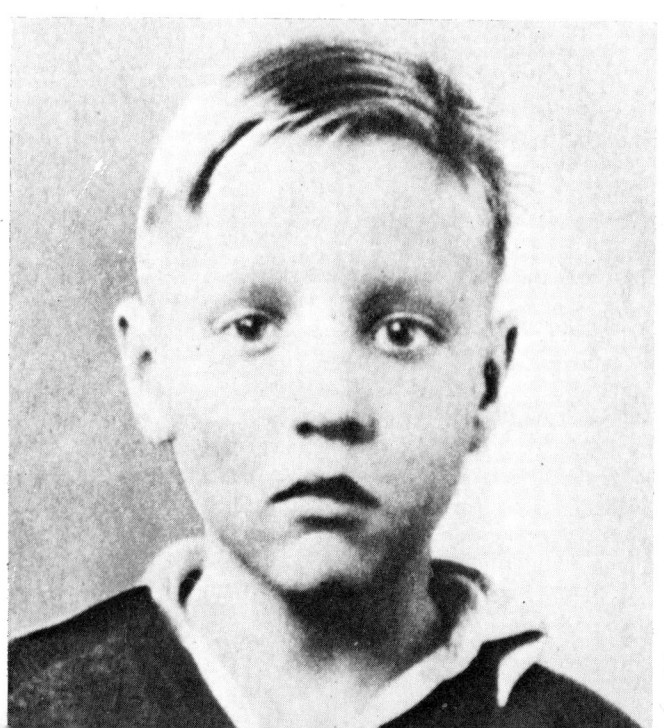

white man a culture he will never acknowledge: it is American Gospel. His parents and his country and the First Assembly of God church are the meaning and marked horizons of his life: there is no other way.

His mother has lived in Lee County all of her life, has five sisters, three brothers, a hard time. Her folks had farmed some, but were otherwise anonymous; just another large underfed family, struggling along. When she met Vernon Presley, a man as poor as she, they had a quick courtship and got married; a romantic endeavour. Her husband was a quiet man, grabbing work where he could, doing his best to get on in this county where work wasn't plentiful at the best of times. From sun-up to sunset he hoed cotton and corn, humped bales, delivered milk, sorted lumber – tried just about everything. So he did the rounds, working here, working there, while his wife climbed from bed in the cold dawn to make breakfast then work in the garment factory – twelve long hours a day. Now the child sees them, is enfolded in their love, but knows nothing of how they survive. His mother embraces him, comforts him, making up for her lost child, soothing this one's clinging fears. He will always be loved.

They have breakfast, the dawn breaks, the day begins; it is Sunday, it is time for church. His mother takes him by the hand, and with a wave to his father walks him down to the small church on Adams Street, where they stand and worship.

It is the Day of our Lord in America in 1943.

Here, and in the fields, and in Beale Street in Memphis, he learns everything he will ever need to know. Black and white are apart, but their cultures have merged, and it is nowhere more obvious than in music. No one will acknowledge it – it is a tacit understanding – but black religion fills white churches in ways that aren't questioned, and this white boy feels black in his bones. The preacher chants fervently, the congregation shrieks "Praise God!" and gazing out at the cottonfields, he hears the noise from the other churches, the raving gospel of the blacks, and takes their rhythm into his bloodstream: when he sings, it's with tainted breath.

The singing comes as naturally as breathing: it is part of his heritage. He lives in the very seat of American folk music where white man and black man swop minor traits. White music is hillbilly, black music is the blues, and some day the two will have to meet. His singing, therefore, is not unusual; it is something he grows with. It is the enthusiasm with which he steps forward to do it and the angelic repose of his face as he utters the words which are remarkable. But he learns early and well. He sings gospel in the churches, folk songs on the porches, and he sometimes sways his body in childish emulation of the niggers he has watched in the fields.

Out of his untutored eyes he observes his parents' withering poverty. They both rise with the dawn and they work hard all day and they don't have too much time for pleasure. His father keeps changing jobs, they have to keep changing houses, endlessly, it seems. He sees his mother's face, feels the tension in her flesh, and he swears one day he'll mend things.

He is at that time of life when the golden haze of childhood must give way to the first buffetings of reality. It is possible that he now sees behind their shielding smiles to the hopelessness lying beyond, to the land's clinging poverty. He sings to his mother when the storms drive them from home; he stands up to sing at school and in church, clear, tremulous, uncertain, with an arresting sincerity that brings tears to the eyes. The songs are bathetic in the country and western vein, tied to blue moons and broken hearts and

trains howling lonesome on those tracks that lead back into history – the songs of deprived folk. Or they are hymns, the spirituals of his church, and they are spun with a high Southern drawl. They are songs at the crossroads.

He's a spoilt child, but he carries it well. Later it will show in contradiction – in his narcissism and in his private humility – but for now it protects him. No one who remembers him will complain of his manners. Sweet and unfailingly polite, quiet and respectful, the hint of rebellion has never touched him. Poor but decent, average at school, he gathers flowers with the other kids, fools around, rarely gets into mischief: an anonymous boy.

Some things, however, are prophetic. At the tender age of ten Elvis Presley is entered for the annual singing contest of the Mississippi-Alabama Fair. He stands up on a chair, sings Red Foley's "Old Shep" and walks off with the five-dollar second prize. He's sung it at school, and to his parents and friends, and he will sing it many times in the future – a favourite song, a real tear-jerker. Some day he will sing it to the masses.

Now he has a guitar in his hands, bought by his parents. He learns to play it by listening to the radio, to the hillbilly stations – to Jimmy Rodgers and Roy Acuff and Ernest Tubb and many others – all of them steeped in country music. He listens to the blues, to the proliferating black men, to Big Bill Broonzy, Otis Span, B. B. King, John Lee Hooker, to Jimmy Reed and Chester Burnett and Booker White – all steeped in "gutter" music. And finally, most always, he sings in church with his folks, and adds spirituals to his broadening repertoire: he picks them up, he plays tricks with them.

The family moves close to Shakerag, Tupelo's black ghetto, and Elvis finds himself at a new school. He is thirteen years

old and is photographed looking threatening in a cowboy suit in front of a painted western landscape. He is, in this photograph, remarkably similar to what he will later become: his eyes are dark-shadowed, his face is lean and narcissistic and a fancy cravat dangles from his neck; he wears a broad belt that is studded and glittering over a pair of real fancy two-toned pants. He is still thirteen years old when the family moves yet again, migrating like the blacks and the other poor whites from the harsh fields to the bright lights of Memphis – the home of the blues.

In Memphis things are bigger, more frightening, more exciting: the alien streets run for miles. There's a new kind of life here, and a new breed of people; there are cinemas and cars and televisions and juke joints, and the kids are slick and strangely restless. The whole world is changing, and while he doesn't comprehend it, he responds to its secret siren call: he yearns for material things.

It is Tennessee's largest city, and though they live near the commercial centre, they are as poor as they ever were before. They have a one-room apartment and share a bath with three families; the walls are ragged with holes and filthy. He goes to a huge school where the strangeness terrifies him, but eventually he adjusts, makes some friends, dates some girls, and starts to change fast without knowing it.

Memphis envelops him.

While both his parents work, his father moving from job to

job, Elvis finds his way about the streets and local customs. He is growing, getting acne, putting grease on his hair, and, though he is still quiet and polite, he is finding the confidence he needs. All the kids now have crew cuts but he wears his hair long, and his sideburns cause more than one fight – he is not slow to swing. Yes, for all his charm, for all his shyness and gentility, he has a violent temper and a certain arrogance that seem totally at odds with his character: he'll cut loose if he's pushed.

They move again. This time they are imprisoned in a three-storey brick building that looms over the leaning shacks of the poorest blacks. Here there are drug stores, beer parlours and factories – and just half a mile away, burning bright in the night, is Beale Street, the home of the blues. There he wanders, past the pimps and the whores, around the winos and the junkies, walking under the bright lights, treading with care, thrilled by the danger, by the strangeness of it all. Blue eyes wide and innocent, drinking it in he listens to the music of the honky-tonks, the beer parlours, the crumbling rooms. The songs are different from his own, they are crude and exciting; they are shocking words growled by these raw, battered blacks to the rhythm of guitars and harmonicas: they are fresh, more vital. And now the music of his childhood, the country songs and the spirituals, are being fused in his mind with what he hears in this street and will make him the future white negro.

Now sixteen years old he buys his clothes in Beale Street – nigger clothes, bright and flashy – he shows a peculiar preference for garish pink and black in the age of the grey flannel suit. Take this, and his long hair and his ever-growing sideburns, place it down in its context, in the Eisenhower years, and you have something outrageous on the loose.

Naturally, he continues to sing, to carry his guitar around. He plays occasionally for his friends, in the school's variety show, at picnics and at the local boys' club – never professional. He isn't showy with it, is more often reluctant – it's just something he does – but once he starts he really gets into it.

The length of his hair now appears to be tied to his desire to become a truck driver like his father. But he's like most other kids: trailing the sweater girls, doubling up to go to movies, taking rides at the fair, throwing balls at milk bottles, longing for a car to go cruising in – a pretty average All American Boy.

The adolescents hang out around the drug stores and juke joints, bored by the past, embalmed by the present, and casting their hazy eyes towards the romantic future. This God-given country is going through its dullest phase, and they can't stand their parents for suffering it. It's excitement they want, and it's excitement they will get, but at the moment they just don't know where to turn. The atmosphere is heavy, desolation clouds the brain; they are affluent and don't know how to spend it – *it's all such a drag*. The girls in their sweaters have bobbed hair and lipstick; the guys – slacks and jumpers, domes neatly crew-cut – play sport. On the radio they listen to Rosemary Clooney and Doris Day, to Vic Damone and Eddie Fisher, and that crap's enough to make you want to weep. There is, it is true, a slight rebellion in the air, most noticeably against parents in grey suits, against all that's static. Yet some things are beginning to happen: Marlon Brando is a brute who sends shivers down the spine, there are people called Beatniks in the most alluring cities and, most important, four-beats-to-the-bar are now drawing crowds back to the dance halls. Yes, changes are coming, but no one quite knows what they are – they only know that they are waiting for the Phoenix to rise from the ashes of post-war mediocrity, for some cool and dangerous and sexy redeemer, some Lazarus.

He is here amongst them and he goes quite unnoticed. He is normal. A growing lad. But that's not to say he's ignored.

In 1953 **Bill Haley** and his Comets have a hit with an item called "Crazy Man Crazy", which words henceforth enter the Language. The changes have started.

Towards the end of his school years Elvis starts working part-time to help out his struggling parents. He works as an usher at Loew's State Theatre, but has to quit when he punches a fellow usher. He works the evening shift at the Marl Metal Products Company which is rough, and makes him fall asleep at school. For this reason he quits again.

His parents are still badly off. They are harassed by the Housing Authority, and they never know when they'll have to move again. The debts are piling up, the kid mows lawns for pocket money, yet no matter how poor they might be, they always look after him. They even go so far as to buy him a Lincoln coupé, which ostensibly is for all of the family, but he uses it. Life sways on a tightrope, but considering the circumstances, he has a very good time – goes to parties, does the bop, hangs on juke boxes, gets his oats – but he

never runs short on the gratitude: he returns all the love he gets.

He leaves school in the June of 1953, gets a factory job, then moves to the Crown Electricity Company. Finally he is a truck driver and he loves it: he is earning his keep. People notice that he likes to comb his hair and that he doesn't give a damn who sees him do it. In fact, so little does he think of the opinions of others that he has his hair trimmed in the beautician's instead of the barber shop.

All life is an accident; so might fame be. Certainly, in his case, he comes by it casually enough.

One of the places the kid drives past in his battered Ford pick-up is the Memphis Recording Service in Union Street. It's a modest offshoot of the Sun Recording Company who specialise in private recordings. The kid has never been in there, but he knows all about it, and he wants to cut a platter for his mother – four dollars, two sides.

It is the summer of 1953. A hot, busy Saturday. Every hustler in Memphis carries a guitar, and thinks he's gonna make it real big when he trembles his tonsils. The office is

Left: Graduation picture taken for Humes High School year book, June, 1953, when Elvis was 18. Above: Elvis in Memphis at 19. Bottom left: Talking to Memphis fans at the age of 20, just before the explosion.

crowded. There must be some tension in the air.

The kid sits in a chair, slicks back his greased hair, and waits his turn. The office manager at this time is one Marion Keisker who has recently been Miss Radio of Memphis. She asks him what he can sing, to which he replies: "Anything." Unperturbed, she then asks him who he sounds like: "I don't sound like nobody", he says. He is shy and polite but he really doesn't know what else to say: it is the innocence of genius.

The kid, now dwelling in the safety of this innocence, goes in to cut the disc for his Ma. He sings one of his favourites – the Ink Spots' "My Happiness" – then he tries "That's When Your Heartaches Begin", a real country tear-jerker.

He doesn't like the sound of his own voice.

This studio is sitting at the crossroads where black music meets white. The owner, Sam Phillips, who loves black music and sells it, is on the lookout for a white man who can sing it: this development must come. If the kid is a genius who will never comprehend it, then Sam Phillips is his reasoning second half. Already Sam has cut records that will go down as classics – though neither he nor his staff are yet to know it. It is even likely that the kid in his studio has been influenced by some of the material: Joe Hill Louis' "We All Gotta Go Sometime", Rufus Thomas' "Bear Cat", perhaps even "Walkin' In The Rain" by the Prisonaires, who sound just like his much beloved Ink Spots. Anyway he is here. And strangely, and contrary to the normal house rules, Miss Keisker decides to put the boy on tape.

"Over and over I heard Sam saying: 'If I could find a white man who had the Negro sound and the Negro feel, I could make a million dollars.' This is what I heard in Elvis, this . . . what I guess they now call 'soul', this Negro sound. So I taped it. I wanted Sam to know."

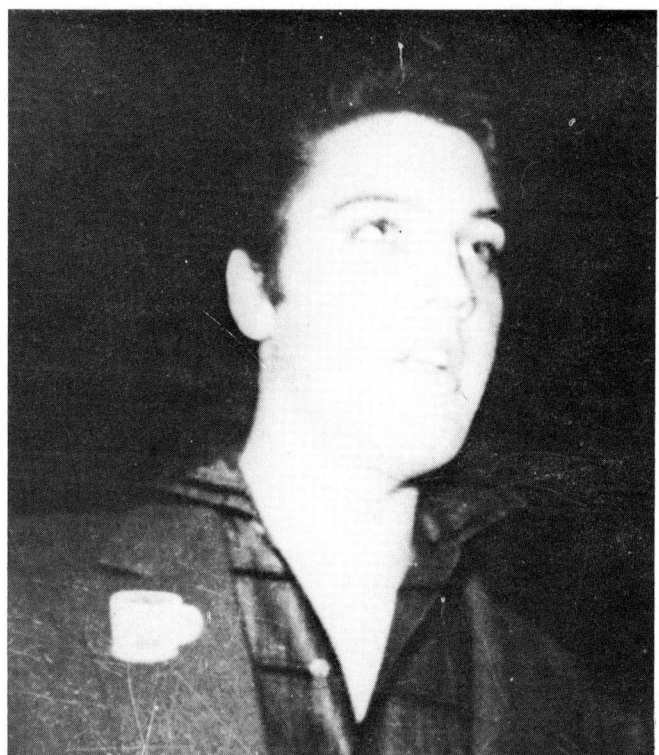

Top left: In Dallas, Texas, 1956. Bottom left and top right: At Union Station, Memphis, 1956, wearing what seems to be the same jacket, but without tie and with a different shirt, about to embark on one of his earlier tours. Above: With a girlfriend, Kate Wheeler, in Dallas, 1956. Note the curled lip and the slick clothes.

The kid finishes and takes his platter home to his mother; his good deed for this day is done. When Sam Phillips hears the tape, he is impressed, but says the boy needs some work. Miss Keisker keeps his address and the phone number of a friend, after which life cruises on in its mellow way. A few months later, on the first Friday of January, 1954, the kid returns to cut another private record. He sings "Casual Love" and "I'll Never Stand in Your Way", then he shuffles out of the studio. He starts learning to be a spark, secretly yearns

Top of page: Two rare photos of Elvis, looking younger than his 21 years at his home at 1034 Audubon Drive, Memphis, in 1956. Above: The Grand Ole Opry. Opposite page: Top left, Elvis with friend George Klein; top right, with dee-jay Dewey Phillips.

to be a singer, and family struggles continue.

About eight months after he has first visited the Memphis Recording Service, they call him up and invite him back to the studio; they have something to try him with.

Sam Phillips has come across a song called ''Without You'' and Miss Keisker thinks the kid might be right for it. He isn't. He is awful. He just can't get it right. They try it once more, then give up in despair, have a coffee break. Sam Phillips asks the kid just what he *can* do, and the kid replies: ''I can

do anything.'' And by way of demonstration he does western, gospel, Dean Martin, Billy Eckstine – you name it, he tries it, he does it. And Sam Phillips falls for it.

What Phillips then does is arrange a meeting between the kid and a skinny guitarist known to all as Scotty Moore. They meet at Scotty's house and when the kid walks through the door he is dressed all in pink but for his white shoes. They horse around for a while and are joined by Bill Black, who isn't at all impressed by this freaky boy. But Bill Black is a bass player, and when they get into the Sun studios, there is

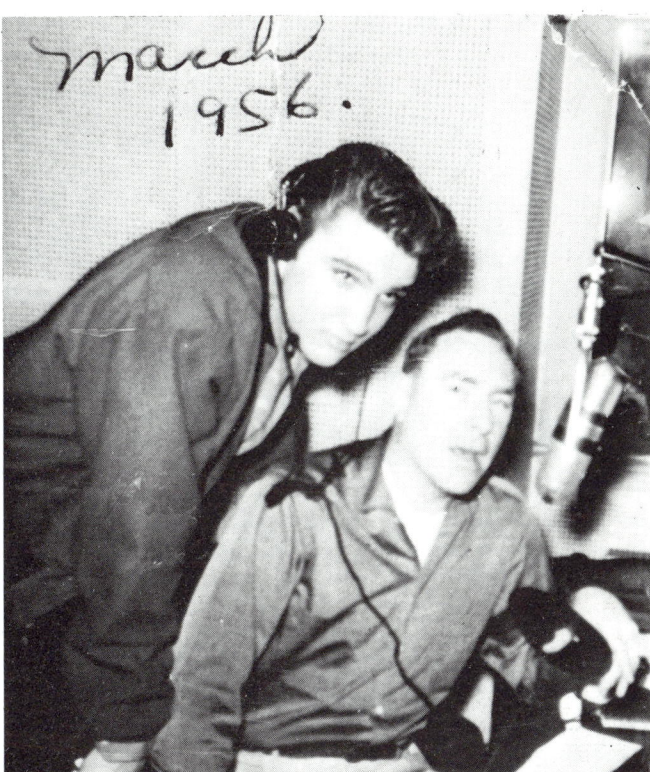

March 1956.

Above: In the Sun Studios, about 1956, with, from left to right, Jerry Lee Lewis, Carl Perkins, Johnny Cash, Marilyn Evans.

just him and Scotty backing Elvis: they will make some extraordinary sounds.

This test session extends into months of hard labour as they work to develop a style. They don't know what they're looking for, and the kid's voice is weird, but for some reason Sam keeps them at it. A couple of times the kid appears with Scotty's band in a local club, but not too many people think it sounds right. They work on. They are not amused. The kid has wild clothes and he's a bit of a looker, but he sure in hell ain't no great singer. Then, after months, out of some intuition, in the hollows of the studio, in that air of desolation, Sam says: "Okay, this is the session." And they turn on the tapes.

The first thing they try is "I Love You Because", a real country weeper so doleful it is more like a dirge. They do four takes of the song and the kid's voice is freaky, pure country but with something else again. He sings high and sings low, sometimes misses a note, and the trembling on occasion seems deliberate. Also, on the first take, he tries a spoken bridge, during which he drawls his words with all the slimy innuendo of a hoodlum inching into the alley. ''Honey,'' he drawls, breaking down any sentiment, ''every time I'm walkin' by your side . . .'' And the contrast is stunning. But it doesn't make a great song. It is pure country and western, an undefiled corn-cob weeper, and it has all the shameless sentimentality of that particular genre. Still, they keep trying. On the second take they cut the spoken bridge and instead add a whistled introduction. The kid sings it much deeper, guitar and bass are more assured, and it is certainly the best of the batch. They try it twice more, but one take is not completed and the fourth version will never be released.

He has cut his first disc.

After this, they turn off the tapes and try some of ''those country-orientated things''. Apparently none of them come to much – most certainly they aren't taped – and they settle for having a break. Sam is back in the control room, the boys are slugging Coke, and the kid takes his guitar in his hands and tries one of his favourites. The song is Arthur Crudup's ''That's All Right Mama'', a jumping blues number, and when the kid cuts into it, singing high and mean, his guitarist and bassist follow suit. The hair of Sam Phillips stands up on his neck : it's electric. He turns on the tapes, makes them run through it again, and that's it. Finally, and almost by accident, he has found what he wants.

The vocal on ''That's All Right Mama'' is high, urgent, desolate and decidedly sensual. It's pure gutter blues with a pounding bass rhythm, but Scotty Moore's guitar retains a country flavour. It is exactly, to the very last note, what Sam Phillips wants. ''On one side we had a country and western

Elvis in the studios, with greased hair and acne, just kicking off on an amazing career. 1956.

ballad with a rhythm and blues feel, and on the other side we had a strictly rhythm and blues song with a slight country feel to it.'' The latter is ''That's All Right Mama''; the former is ''Blue Moon of Kentucky''. When they cut ''That's All Right Mama'' they need something to back it, and finally, four days later, they find something. The first take of ''Blue Moon'' is a brief, medium-tempo, country rocker with a strong and assured vocal treatment. At the end of it, Scotty runs humorously down the chords, that kid takes a nervous breath, and Sam Phillips, with a laugh, says, ''Fine, man! Hell, that's *different!* That's a *pop* song!'' But they tape another version and this one is much faster, with an extraordinarily driving and eccentric vocal that turns the whole thing inside out. This track it is that will back ''That's All Right Mama'', and both tracks form a remarkable debut: black music and white music at long last have joined at the crossroads.

It is the Year of our Lord in America in 1954.

2

*"His key is precise, intuitive knowledge of who he is
and what he's projecting on stage. His consistency
is absolute."*
— Morgan Ames, High Fidelity

The restless children of America now see standing before them the product of their most secret dreams. He is over six foot tall, his hair is greasy and long, he has blue eyes and a curling, self-mocking lip. He comes on real easy, as if he's always owned the stage, grins at his boys as if it's all some kind of joke, then picks up his guitar and lightly strums it, pretending to play. This boy is no country yokel. Rather he's Flash Harry, a dreamy-eyed dude, and he knows it and knows how to carry it. His instincts are sound.

He sees them. He grins at them. It is all they need. They prostrate themselves.

No one ever knows where he picked up the confidence, the charisma, the sublime public ease. He can bite his fingernails, tap his feet on the floor and drum his fingers in acute nervous spasms – but once in the spotlight he is confident, he knows he can do it. The young man has learnt quickly, all America is his, and when he leans toward the mike, when his fingers caress it, they all sense that he's into some private dream, willing to share it. He is Lazarus arisen from the ashes of their boredom: a cool, dangerous and very sexy animal who will transport them briefly to Heaven.

He is called Elvis Presley.

The rise to local fame is a gradual acceleration which for most struggling artists would be lightning but for him is a snail's crawl. He has played on flat trucks and in schools and in stadiums; he has driven across the South, across Texas, to the nation; he has lived through those long nights with the salt of rejection and he has got himself a few pink cadillacs: he grins crookedly, self-mocking.

He leans forward like an animal, legs apart, body braced, the guitar hanging loose like a weapon; he purrs like a big cat.

Above left: The slim, smiling cowboy is famed country singer Hank Snow, pictured with Elvis during a Grand Ole Opry tour. The "live" shots on these pages are amongst the earliest ever taken (1955). Bottom right: Elvis relaxes by playing the piano with his parents.

They scream, writhe, wet the seats, tear their hair and claw at their own faces with sweaty hands – he enjoys it. His lips twist in a grin as he reaches out for the mike stand, fingers sliding slowly down it, then curling around and taking hold, rocking it gently. He growls just a little, flicks the hair from his eyes, lets his heavy-lidded gaze burn up the front rows, raises his left hand.

The hysteria is immediate and total.

When he finally starts to sing he knows just how to do it, since the tapes he has put down for the Sun Record Company are the most remarkable ever made by a white man. Like many a great actor, he has worked by his instincts, turning up to record with nothing prepared and then sweating for hours to find material, to find the right approach. Nothing in this particular line comes easy to him: it is all a huge sweat. But the results which are sparse in these first early days make up in quality what they are lacking in quantity: they are gold in the wilderness. He takes pure country songs and then rapes them with the blues; he takes the blues and refines them into pop songs. This, in itself, would be quite an achievement, but it isn't what makes a man myth. No, what he has given them, these bored, restless children, is a raw and untutored sensuality, a first hint of freedom.

He stands in the spotlight and he gives them what they want because it's all that he ever learnt to do. He heard it in the churches, in fields and on the porches; he saw it at revivalist meetings and in the black men of Beale Street. So he sways his body, shakes a leg, rolls his groin, does it first slow and easy, a slithering come-on, then quickens up, turns almost epileptic, and makes love to his guitar. This instrument, in fact, will soon be but a prop: a symbol of arrogant contempt, the first real modern phallus.

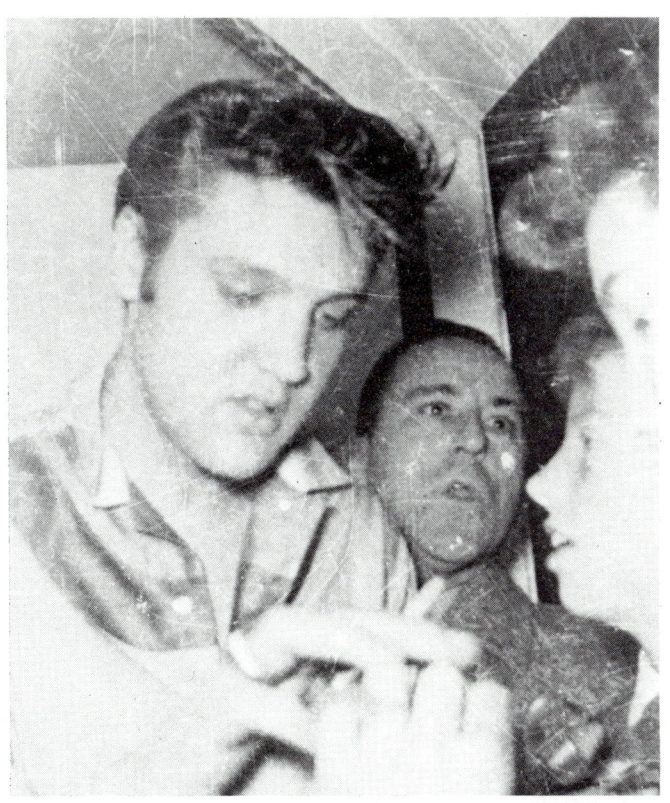

A return to Tupelo on 25 September, 1956, to perform once more in the Mississippi-Alabama Fair where at 10 years old he first sang ''Old Shep''. Soon after this he would purchase Graceland, 3764 Highway 51, South Memphis (below).

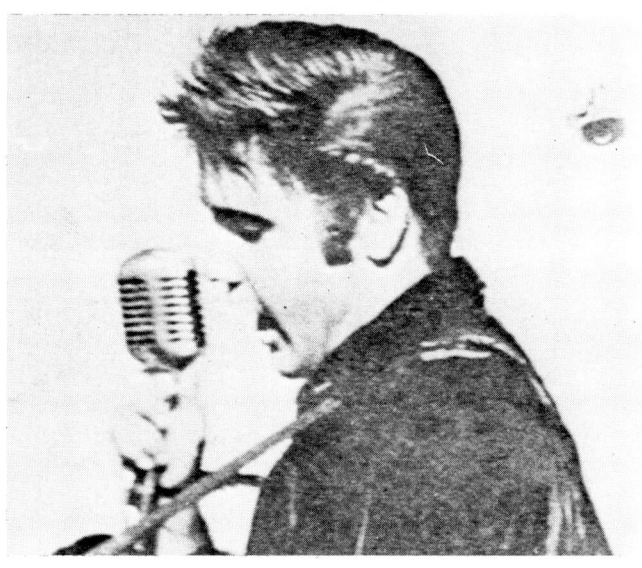

At first he eases into his performance with a sly, wicked charm. Walking on without prelude he will lean towards the mike, let loose with the lop-sided grin, burn them up with his eyes. Then, just to tease, he will start with a ballad, leaning close to the mike, almost kissing it, breathing over it, his long eye-lashes modestly lowered, almost effeminate. It's a beautiful trick, a sublime delaying tactic: he will hold them in the palm of his hand until he's ready to jump. The guitar, very early, becomes no more than an accessory, an item to toy with, a symbol, something to stroke. And his voice, in such ballads, will be close to a groan, a strangled sound, strangely orgasmic, drawing them in. He knows what he is doing. The tension is rife. And he will dangle his left hand like a limp, sodden leaf – then twitch, just a little, and watch the fireworks.

This developing knowledge of the psychology of the audience is something he will never lose. He will watch them with his eyes, and with his arrogant grin, but his instinct is what he'll depend on. So, after the ballad, and sensing their tension, he will turn slightly away, mumble out a few words, let the honey of his voice and his deep Southern accent charm them into a soft romantic haze – then he'll cut loose.

In the earliest shows it is ''Good Rockin' Tonight'' and the throb of Bill Black's bass will set the mood. The kid will shake his left leg, smack one hand on a thigh, jerk his shoulders as if in a spasm, rock back on his heels. The audience goes wild: they have witheld too long; now release is here. He grins, shakes his head, throws the hair back from his eyes, then howls the first word like a hound on the prairie – a long, drawn out, spine-chilling, ''Weeeelllll . . .'' His rendition of this number is a blatant overlaying of brute lust on pure country corn: it is Brando gone pop. He invites them out back of the barn: there's good rockin' tonight. It is pure come-hither-baby and it works like a charm because the way he phrases ''rock'' means something else – and you didn't discuss that.

The changes come so fast they're overwhelming, a cyclone of harassment. In 1955 he starts touring with the Grand Ole

When not being moody out back of Graceland (above), Elvis was being scandalous on stage. The performance shown here and overleaf was in New York, 1956.

and unusually handsome, he has "a Latin quality . . . beautiful, smouldering eyes, long dark brown hair and sideburns". His hips begin to undulate, his head whips up and down, and he seems altogether to be in some sort of trance, sometimes smacking the guitar instead of playing it, an evangelical chanter. Suddenly it isn't the Grand Ole Opry as they've ever understood it; it's like nothing they have ever seen before. The adults are revolted, other performers think it's crazy, but the kids in the audience are pop-eyed and start to go wild. Yes, he bring the house down, and Hank Snow, who tries to follow him, is shamefully booed off the stage . . . thereafter, no one tries it.

By late 1956 he already has his own show and things are considerably different. He plays the Dallas Cotton Bowl and the cops are so worried they erect a ten-foot fence around the stage. The kid, The Pelvis, makes his entry into the field in a new and gleaming Lincoln white convertible, waving a friendly hand. The audience, which at this gig numbers a good 26,000, goes berserk before he opens his mouth – the formula is set. Now, of course, he has progressed beyond mere country and western, has discarded the mandatory cowboy outfit. Flash Harry he is and Flash Harry he'll be, climbing out of the convertible with his lop-sided grin to reveal, in his modest manner, "a billiard-table green coloured coat, black trousers, pleated white shirt, black tie, snow-white boots that zip up the side, huge cufflinks and a striped cummerbund around the top of his pants . . ." No horse shit: he's changing. Then he runs through his hits, does his Dracula bit, and leaves

Opry, a hillbilly show covering the east. He plays in the arena in Norfolk, Virginia, and he's just one more country yodeller in a cowboy outfit with a guitar in his hands, looking lonesome. There's a long red silk scarf knotted loosely around his neck, a round-brimmed black hat pushed far back on his head, quite exotic, framing pale face and dark hair. Tall, lean

them wasted with a version of "Hound Dog" that would shame a burlesque show.

Naturally, at the gate, one ear cocked to the hysteria, his new manager, Colonel Parker, heavy and benign, is selling Beanie hats, photographs, records and other Elvis souvenirs – since it isn't just a pop show, it's a carnival, and it always will be.

Not too many months later, in the huge Mosque theatre in Richmond, he's still flashy but much better groomed. His body has filled out, he looks sleek and prosperous, and his hair has gone more dark with grease, his sideburns more prominent. In the view of at least one fan, he has "gorgeous, thickly lashed, velvety blue eyes, and peaches and cream complexion" as well as "great poise and distinction". He wears a stage shirt of white silk trimmed in lace, a black suit cut from an extremely rich material, and a pair of black patent leather slippers. Later still, growing ever more flamboyant, he will wear a specially tailored suit of "soft, pliable leather, impregnated with gold . . . the silver lapels and trouser stripes

Kansas City, 1956, with Bill Black on bass, Scotty Moore on guitar, J. D. Fontana on drums. Hysteria prevailed.

encrusted with brilliants'', all of which ''sparkle and shimmer'' in the lights of the stage. They shimmer most particularly when he does his special thing, which is to take hold of the mike, pull it down at an angle, then gyrate his pelvis in an extraordinarily violent bump and grind while his right fist swathes through the hot air: a blatant, sadistic rape.

These are the first solo performances and they're something to see, but within a couple of years he has extended them. By 1957 he has taken his own measure, and he knows that by scaring the sheep he will capture the lambs. So, he is outrage-

ous, he is totally wild, he is something from the backwoods of the uncultured American South just come out of the trees for some plunder: this feat is stupendous. He is still indefinable – his background so pious – yet he works with an instinct that can only be genius to contradict every *more* of his breeding: he's a nice boy gone ape.

This persona is an inspired piece of *kitsch*, a remarkable invention. He has the looks of a hoodlum, yet he talks like a gentleman; on-stage he's a maniac, yet off-stage he's a saint; he sums up for his fans the revolt against adults, yet he loves his own folks with a shameless love – the controversy is exquisite.

''I never thought my performing style was wicked. *Wicked?* I don't even smoke or drink!''

Nor does he. He says yes-sir and no-ma'am, sings hymns, collects teddy bears, eats hot dogs, hamburgers and popcorn, never touches the demon brew. A monster on stage, his real life style is a hymn to youthful decency, a catalogue of the mundane and trivial, so ''normal'' it's ludicrous. He's a devotee of the most plastic verities of American life; he dates only nice girls, only takes them to the movies, never enters a night club or bar, doesn't gamble or smoke. He loves his parents, worships God and God's country, is grateful for everything he's been given – a most loyal son. Yet once in the spotlights, with his sharp eyes highlighted, he sneers and beseeches, seduces and surrenders, spits defiance at everything good children should revere, is no less than the sinner incarnate, the hooligan king. He is the most contradictory image to be placed on the American landscape – and he's marvellous copy.

''I don't know what happens to me when I sing. Maybe it's the music, the song, the crowd or something deep inside me, but to the rock 'n' roll beat I have to move my hands, feet, knees, legs, my head – everything. There were attacks on my singing style in the papers – but I felt that I could sure live them down.''

He doesn't live them down – doesn't even bother trying –

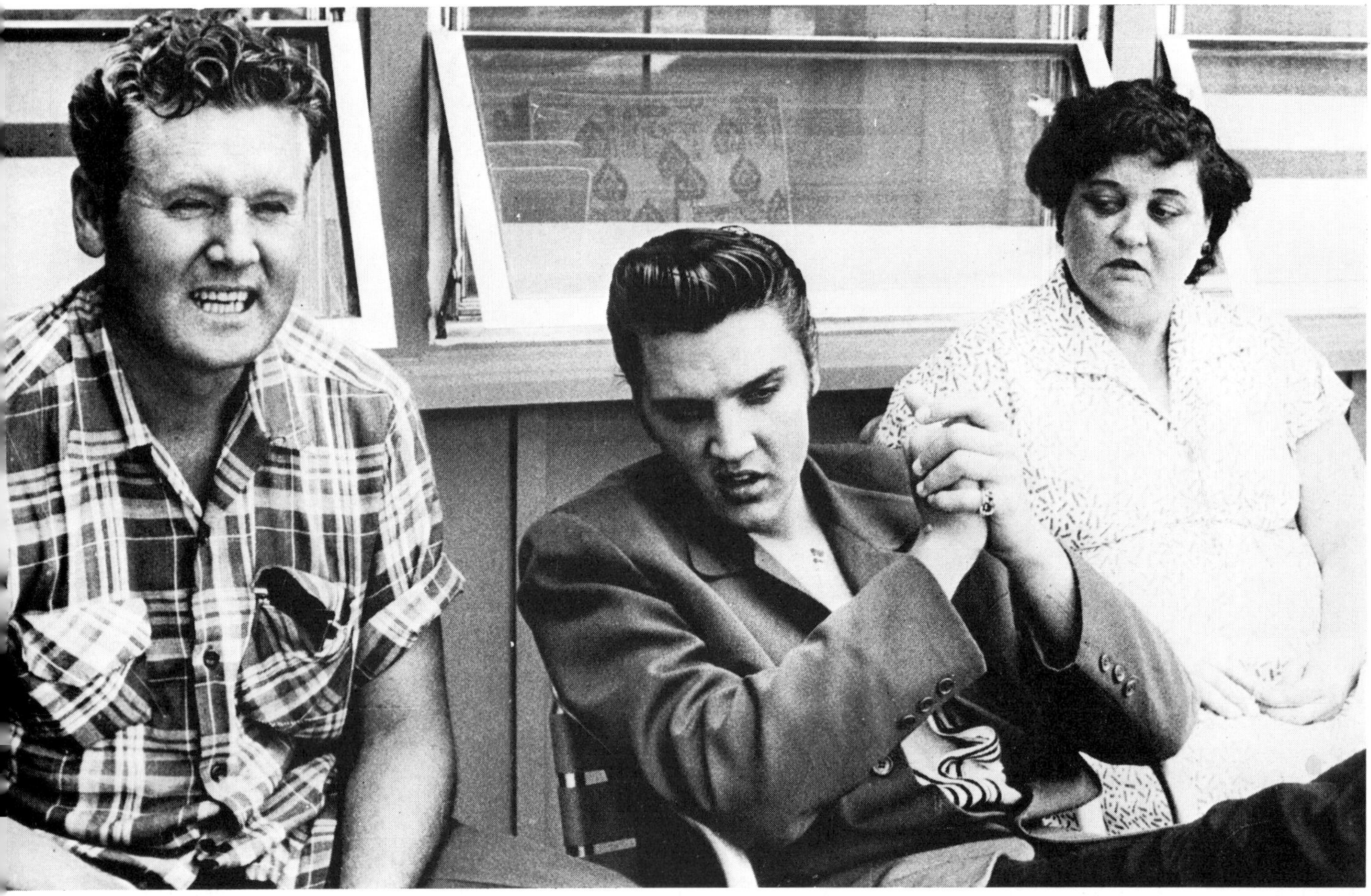

Top: With his mother and father in 1957. Above: Playing cops 'n' robbers back of Graceland. Opposite: 1957.

lighted in the spotlights which pierce through the stark blackness when he stands on his toes, makes his hands like two claws, pops his eyes, his curled lip cruel, and snarls just like a vampire – pure evil, a rare treat.

He does "Heartbreak Hotel" when the main lights are turned down, when the spotlights cut into his blue eyes, his lean wicked features. He bends his left leg, supports himself on the right, and then throws out his arms in appeal, like a man crucified. *"Well since mah baby left me/I've found a new place t' dwell/It's down at the end of Lonely Street at/Heartbreak Hotel."* His voice is desolate, raging, standing out on its own, punctuated by a guitar so savage it's like a chop on the neck. Then he swivels his hips, the mike caught between his thighs, head back and eyes closed, a sublimely tortured pose, and groans, almost grunts, monosyllabic and wracked, *"And I'm a so lonely, baby/I'm a so lonely/And I'm a so lonely/Ah could die."* It is blatant theatrics, an acting out of the lyrics, a visualised extension of his voice, of the bleak, surrealistic words. When he gets to the bellhop, to the desk clerk dressed in black, he runs his left foot up the back of his right leg, slides one hand on a thigh, leans well back, his mouth open and howling: a wild beast in pain. It is more than they can bear – they are out of their seats – they are rushing for the stage and as the cops push them back he already has gone on to something else, crouching over, hands flailing. The guitar of Scotty Moore takes a mean, lashing break, and the kid is right in there, almost kissing the floor, his body shaking to the rhythm, in a dream, in a fever, then whipping around fast as it finishes, pointing straight at the fans. *"So if yoh baby leaves ya/And ya got a tale to tell/Jest take a walk down Lonely*

instead he plays up to the avalanche of condemnation by becoming even more outrageous than before: black shirts and white ties, phosphorescent pink socks, gold lamé suits; his eyes are pencilled in and his fair hair dyed black to add demoniac qualities to his rough romantic good looks. In his stage act, these attributes are given prominence, high-

Street to/Heartbreak Hotel . . .'' Now slurring his words, a deliberate masquerade, he curls himself around the mike, starts the stroking and guttural groaning, that sly suggestion of pillow talk . . . *"And am a so lonely, baby/Am a so lonely/ And am a so lonely/Ah could die . . ."* Moaning and purring, breathing heavily, sometimes sighing, just rolling on the boards, very casual, calculating, repeating *"Ah could die, ah could die"* as if in orgasm.

Opposite page: Police protection is now a necessity. Below left: Back stage with fan, Miss Vera Tschechowa, 1957.

After this there is nothing he can't do; his freedom is total. In the very early days Bill Black fooled with his bass to add novelty to a straight country act – but all that is now past. Up there is one man, a young demon, a beauty, who will straddle the mike, shake it loose between his thighs, stroke its flank as he lies on the floor, give it head, give it spasms. The cops are in the pits, but for once in their lives they're more wary of the man on the stage than they are of the audience: a wild man, a maniac, a highly paid lout. And dear Jesus, he's corrupting their kids – and the kids love him for it.

The whole thing is a pure hallucination, a spotlit, chaotic dream. From his own vantage point he sees a white haze of bright light, the pure eye of the sun, huddled masses, a shimmering blackness. But they, in the theatre, in the cramped sweaty seats, are looking up at a glittering idol, a golden young god who is the very essence and meaning of glamour – excitement concentrated. This response is part sexual, part romantic, and always self-willed. But he, this young Elvis, will dredge

from their souls every last ounce of fleeting frustration, each singular hope. And this sense of unreality, this well-rehearsed fantasy, is given credence by the crowds, by the darkness, by the blinding lights, and by the monstrous noise that clamps down on the brain and cuts out all extraneous matter: it's a trip through the subconscious.

"People want to know always why I can't stand still when I'm singing. Some people tap their feet, some people snap their fingers, some people just sway back and forth. I just sort of do them all together, I guess . . . I watch my audience and listen to them and er . . . er . . . and I know that we're all getting something out of our system and none of us knows what it is. The important thing is we're getting rid of it and nobody's getting hurt."

His words spiral over the airwaves and into print; a whole world opens out for TV panelists: this subject will feed them.

Yes, this nice boy in his innocence is corrupting our children, encouraging hooliganism, making whores of our young girls, turning nice young men into wild brutes who spit in your face. It's a sin, it's a shame, it's indecent, and it's quite Un-American.

But he's a valuable release for all the tensions that beset the adolescent: he'll distract them from worse crimes. He is there, after all, with James Dean and Marlon Brando. He is violent, surly, rebellious and sexual, but beneath it all he is sensitive, all-aching, a lonely child . . .

He is, in short, a common identity.

He picks himself up from the stage floor, all dishevelled, sweat pouring, and taking up his guitar, he wipes his brow and turns solemnly towards his audience, just laid low by "Mystery

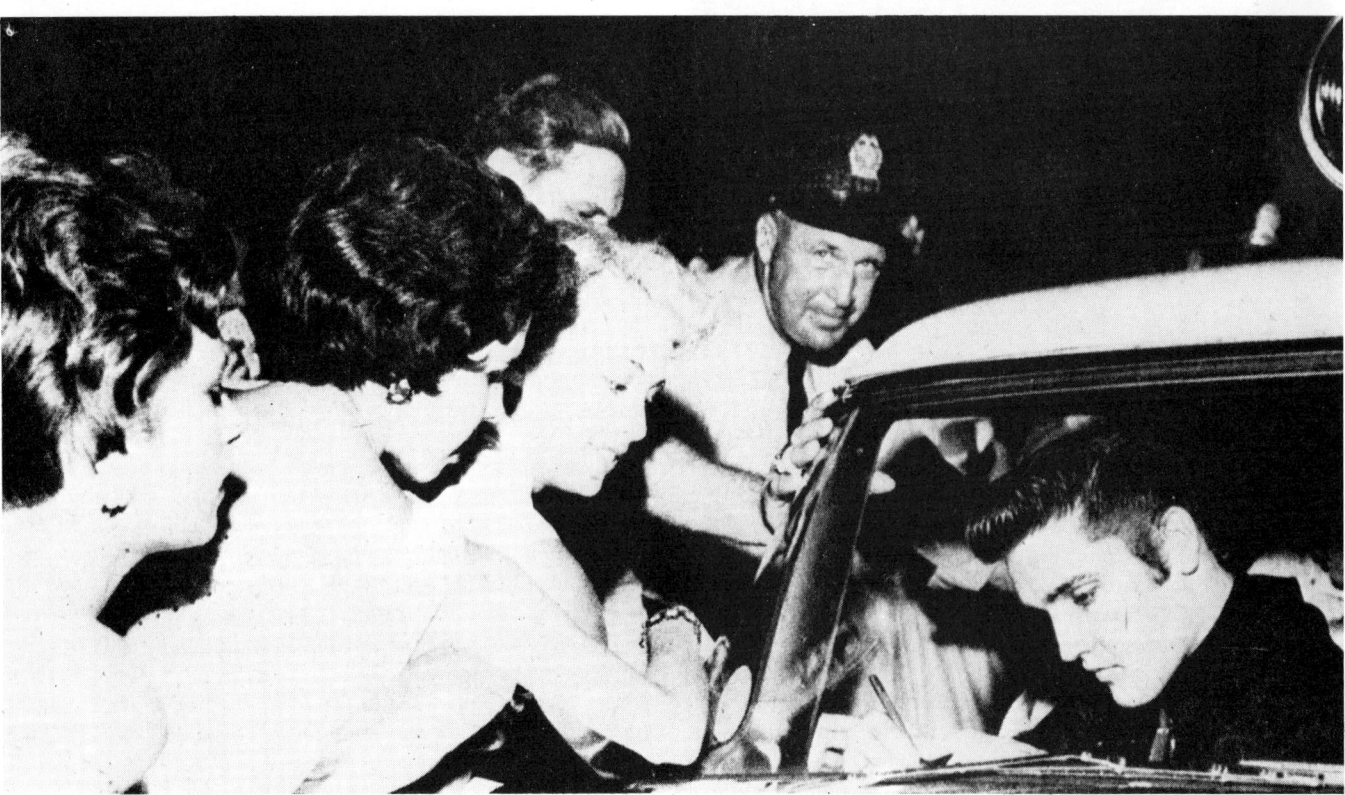

Dressed in black and demoniac on stage, off stage he is sweet when signing autographs. Opposite page: A rare shot of Elvis with Colonel Parker and one brand new car – a gift from the legendary manager. Overleaf: The fireball rocks on.

Train'' or ''Long Tall Sally'', now one huge, black, writhing mass in the dark pit of the theatre. Many young girls in that great age of yearning are now seeing all their dreams fulfilled, their secret guilts understood. And the young men — some look just like him, and others sneer and want to get up there, want to smash him to pieces. Yes, he is something much more than a crooner: he looks as mean and as rough as your local redneck and they don't like him threatening them this way — so they hate him, they ape him. And he, who always watches his audience and listens, gives everyone just a little of what they need.

He now takes hold of the mike, offers one solemn stare, lowers his long-lashed dark eyes and bows his head. This moment is sombre, all stillness, almost religious. While they are dazed by the violence of his previous number, he sings, near to a whisper, a ballad or gospel song. It is total audacity, pure instinctive histrionics, and the contrast is so brutal that the audience seems staggered, sinks slowly back, reclining, collapsing, hypnotised by his reverence, his intense, tortured face, his slow, snakelike swaying, his lonesomeness, his brimming sincerity. It is all too much (he's so violent, so gentle) and they surrender to pure sensual pleasure, enclosed in their dreams.

The regional flavour of his talent is most evident when he brings on the gospel. He sings it like he's standing at the altar of the church, now heavy with vibrato, now almost falsetto, bending notes, flattening notes, pouring out black, evangelical passion. This is the music of this country and no boy who can sing it can possibly be as bad as he seems: every mother could love him.

Some mothers do, but some mothers don't, because what he represents is a threat to their daughters, to their sheltered lives. And not only their daughters, to their wandering sons, who come in nights in gaudy clothes, hair long and greasy, to stare at them with moody eyes. Promiscuity is rife: the very bone and moral fibre of the age is being smashed by this hoodlum. What's happening to the country — you might indeed ask — when such indecency is allowed on the stage? We just don't understand it.

The schism between parents and children is now almost complete. The old world has died, a new world is in the making, and the casualties are falling on both sides. Now young folk are affluent, they are restless and jaded, and they need their

own leaders to guide them – they want their own world. Politics turn them off, hearth and home are just jokes, and ambition has done nothing for their parents but leave them sucked dry. So, disowning this, they will live for the moment, for the hot glittering instant that has no tomorrow, for excitement, existentialist thrills, success now or never. Yes, they want slick clothes and fast cars and a common identity, and they see it in Brando with his violence and sexuality – and in Elvis with his pink cadillacs, his flash, his freedom.

Everyone gets a little of what they need; he is always most generous. And later he comes in heavy with his new kind of songs, those Big City crushers. He is with RCA and those boys in Noo Yawk, guys who know how to foster an image and write around what they have. The songs are commercialised rhythm and blues, witty and vicious, primitive and exciting, geared to that sense of rebellion that has blown like a hurricane across America; aggressive songs, sexy songs. They will no longer write of blue moons and autumn leaves, of dancing in the dark and holding hands. The Hillbilly Cat, the King of Western Bop, is now Elvis the Pelvis and he'll prove it with bone-hard material. He will sing about sweat, about the fevers of love, about blue suede shoes and gleaming black cadillacs, about mean dirty thrills and raw women: he will sing of the hidden life. *"I want you, I need you"*, he groans. *"Make me thrill with delight."* Then he challenges with panache and a real sense of power: *"Don't you step on mah blue suede shoes"*, and he does it with his head back, the left leg like a piston, the guitar slanting upward like a phallus exploring, one hand on a thigh, pelvis rocking, hair flaying his face. Then he drops to his knees, takes the mike along with him, runs his hand right along it and quivers while the shrieks fill his ears. And somewhere behind him, in the black of the stage, his musicians and vocal group will lay down a sound that is almost blocked

out by the bedlam. The place is hysterical.

He is banned more than once and they love him because he's dangerous, because he's wild and untamed, and because, behind this, lies the clean Southern boy who loves his mother, his country and his God. And though they'll never admit it, it's the saint behind the beast that allows them this ephemeral indulgence: he is after all loveable.

The first shadows of mythology now encircle him, enshrine him in Holy clouds. His life style is the style for a whole generation, and it's stretching out over the world. In the jungles of Thailand there are Elvis Presley sweaters; in Japan he is a monstrous industry. His voice is unmistakeable, his face fills sundry dreams, and his first name is part of the language, a new word for the cool. He walks on the waters of a fame so complete that it doesn't leave room for human traits: he is God-like, inviolable.

Somewhere within this the Tupelo child has disappeared, the Memphis boy has been laid in his grave, the bright deity created. He is so famous as to be quite removed, a pure abstract vision.

Remorselessly determined, he always gives a performance that is never less than total. He never accepts *No* for an answer: he will not let them rest. Witnesses to these performances will later testify that he never lost sight of the audience, would never release them. No, he played them by the minute, by each silence and shriek, and he never let up until he had them in his palm, until they lay there before him in utter surrender, were close to the edge of delirium, near out of control. Only then, and not before, would he attempt to level them out – with his self-mocking humour, his sense of the ridiculous, his basic and healthy grasp of the joke, of his own selfish pleasure. And this hint of remove, this

latent lack of conviction, would stand him in good stead in the future, on the day of his resurrection.

"Well, we're gonna do a little ol' bit here . . . er . . . little ol' thing we just recorded in *Noo* York . . .er . . . you know, don't git hysterical down there, kid, ah mean *New* York . . . er . . . a place, you know, with *sidewalks* . . . yeah, well, this little ol' bit here, it's a very tender ballad . . . er . . . real *sweet* song 'bout a gal I know . . . er . . . nice kid . . . just like you, honey, just like you . . . and I says to her . . . I says . . . I mean, breathin' *real* close . . . I says . . .''

And he braces his legs, leans over real low, curls his fingers around the mike and gently rocks it, just teasing, eyes mocking. He grins, the lip curls, it is pure humorous sadism, and they shriek, they howl, they come out of their seats; they are clawing at their own faces, and holding on to each other, tears streaming down their cheeks, some wet between the legs, knowing what he's going to do, hardly daring to believe it, because he's shattered the world with it, stripped away their minds, and it's a number put over like nothing has ever been done before: a real old gutter blues turned into pure wild aggression, a Kowalski song, a thunderous raver, white primitive brilliance. So he starts crouching low,

44

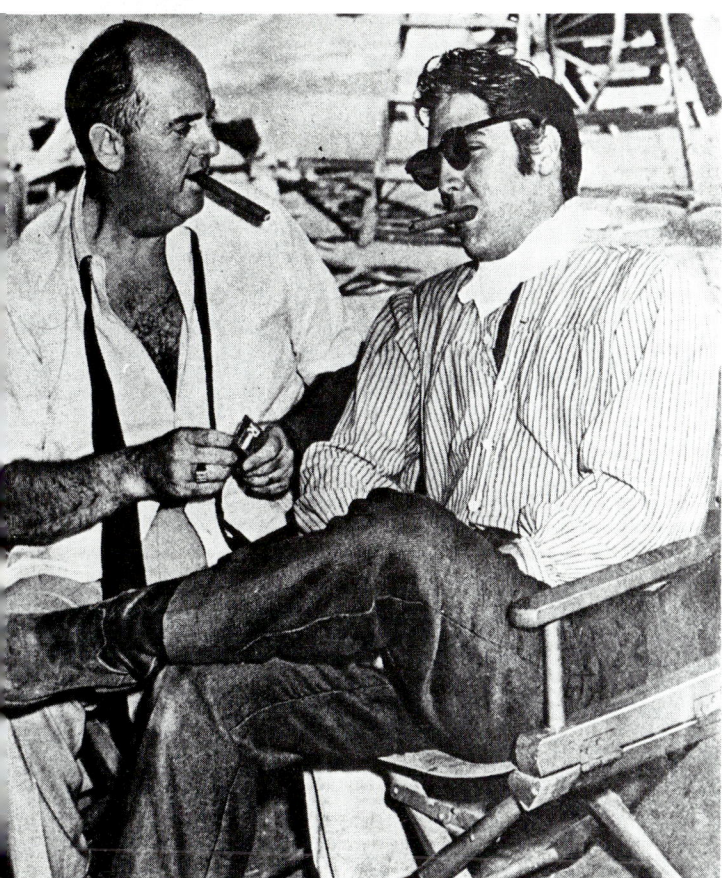

Left: Elvis sharing a cigar with Colonel Parker. On stage he was someone else again: a demon unleashed.

45

He performs a bump 'n' grind and makes defiant gestures. Nevertheless, he will soon be a tamed man. It is 1958.

breathing into the mike, running fingers up and down it, almost hugging it, swallowing it, and then purrs, and then growls, and then laughs and starts again – and then suddenly drops down to one knee with fist outstretched and howls this abuse in their faces, this back-handed slap.

Once hated by the Southerners for singing like a black man, he now sounds like a slave in the bear pit: his shrieks are pure rage. "Hound Dog" is the ultimate song of contempt, and he never fails to close the show with it, whipping his audience. They lie back in their seats as his voice flays their minds, as his clawing hands seem to strip them bare, his groin a pure challenge. Then he does a bump and grind, slides one hand down a thigh, tugs his ears, pops his eyes and looks monstrous – they squeal and collapse.

He will sometimes work this song to its ultimate limits, doing as many as sixteen choruses, each building on the last, each leading the audience to new levels of hysteria. He is

now safely shielded behind blue ranks of cops, behind clubs and some pistols and heavy men – a president's bodyguard. And he does truly need it, forever after will, because what fills these theatres, these stadiums and auditoriums, is something not easily controlled: a frenzied, amorphous beast. And he knows it, and feels it, and responds to its call, raging at it with his voice, with his sly sense of mockery, with his matchless ability to pull them from their seats, take their latent sexuality and whip it to a frenzy that will only be released in pain and tears.

It can't be done with publicity – it is much more than that – it is a mystery of the ages, it's real, it *exists*. No one knows where it comes from, what hidden strength wills it, but in some it can not be denied, and in him never is. So he falls to his knees, thrusts his groin in their faces, crawls over the stage like a snake on its belly, convulses, jerks upright, twists back to his feet, leans into the mike, works in spasms, releasing it all. Yes, he sings sixteen choruses and he thrashes himself mercilessly, tries to drag from himself, perhaps even simulates, the common passions of his juvenile audience, shares with them this mystery. And when he's finished, he doesn't bow, never comes back for an encore, is just rushed away shivering, sometimes crumbling from exhaustion, and disappears before they know what has hit them.

They then smash up the theatres.

He had wanted to be big and he is big – there will never be bigger. He has come at a time when the whole world seems stale, when the young are suppressed and want freedom – and this he has given them. Having, in a real sense, just ripped off the black man, he will now just as unconsciously

pay back his debt by opening the doors to black music, by encouraging the marriage. After this the world will never be the same: there is a general awakening. White kids will ape black kids – their walk, their jive talk – and black music and literature will flood over the land to change cultural and class boundary lines, to make visible the invisible man. Yes, he does this, and he does it alone – and of everyone involved he will be the last person to understand it . . . after all, he is just entertaining.

He sings like a black man, but Dean Martin is his idol and it's Martin's world he now will pursue. He will learn to be a crooner, to be smooth and romantic, to leaven this brew with some dry wit and urbanity, to take Hollywood and conquer the silver screen – to be everything he's dreamed of. How ironic, then, to have changed the whole world because he wanted to be what the new world despises: a common entertainer, a ''star'', pure factory fodder.

So his voice will change and his act become subdued; so he will live in a mansion, in a house with a swimming pool. And like others he admires, he will surround himself with body-guards and with yes-men who will never speak out, who will always congratulate. And in doing this, he blindly puts himself, without resistance, even willingly, into the hands of the promoters, the fat-bellied salesmen. And they will shadow his eyes and put paint on his lips, cake his face and smooth out his rough features: they will make him look plastic. And once they've done this, they will package him and sell him to the larger masses huddled around the globe. And he will accept it saying yes-sir and no-ma'am – a most obedient Southern boy.

47

3

*"That's how you're selling me, isn't it? A monkey in a
zoo. Isn't that what you want?"*
– Deke Rivers (Elvis Presley) in Loving You

Elvis Presley is processed. Bought off Sun Records by the huge RCA company, the welcome mat laid down before him, he is now a big star. At the first recording sessions at RCA Nashville, the studio is bigger, there's more money to burn, and he's surrounded by a tougher, more cunning breed. While he sits at the piano, while he fiddles with the drums, he is observed by Colonel Parker, by his assistant Tom Diskin, by Steve Sholes, by some cronies, by the representative of Hill and Range Songs, by Freddie Bienstock, the manager of his own music company – all watching pure gold being processed.

Now the writers are under contract, the dubs come in huge piles; the whole thing is one huge operation, where nothing is left to chance. He tries take after take, he works long days

and often through the night until everyone's shattered. The results are stupendous, all monsters, all destined for fame: ''Heartbreak Hotel'', ''Hound Dog'', ''Blue Suede Shoes'', ''Don't be Cruel'' – these and many others are created in these days and most of them will go down as classics – commercial but unique.

The voice is now extraordinary, the most versatile in pop, and there isn't a trick that he can't use, no tactics evade him. Now he has a vocal group, four men, the Jordanaires, and they weave some sweet harmonies behind him, softening the sound. He uses lots of echo, slaps his hands on his guitar, thumps his knees, bangs the studio walls, makes some strange ''slapping'' rhythms. He is anguished and sexy and contemptuous by turns; he is humorous and aggressive and

51

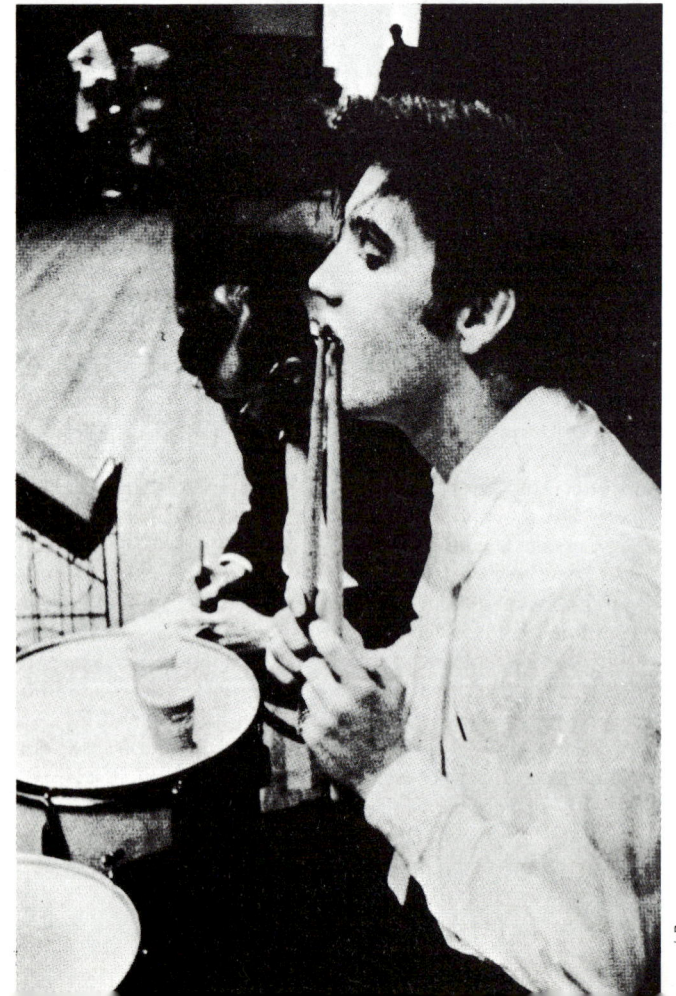

Recording sessions at RCA Nashville, 1956. Top left opposite page: Elvis, watched by Bill Black, talks to the Jordanaires. Top left of this page: Scotty Moore, seated behind a vigorous Elvis, looks exhausted. Top right: Elvis and the Jordanaires run through a rehearsal. Overleaf: First publicity stills from 1956.

malign – never embarrassed. He shows sweat on every track that he makes, lets it ooze from the grooves, has it dripping from his tonsils, bathes the words in it. His productions, indeed, have the raw and guileless intimacy of the greatest lovers and fools known to man: they are quite irresistible.

The first publicity photographs are an uneasy mixture, since his new owners aren't sure what he is and are not yet confident in handling him. The "action" shots are ludicrous: he is posed with arms outstretched, leaning over the guitar, both legs bent – a stiff, grotesque doll. He wears a red windbreaker, white open-necked shirt, black trousers and white gold-buckled sneakers. His eyebrows are painted in, his face is smoothed out, and the background is washed-out yellow:

a representative lunacy. They are better on the head shots, tackling every persona. During one particular session, using very sharp highlights, they dress him up in a flowing green shirt, make his hair stiff with laquer, and take shots that could cover each image, and will in time do so. In one he looks clean-cut, almost Byronic, his eyes moody and piercing in his young, boyish face, the sneer totally removed to show tender lips: a romantic girl's dream. By contrast, in another, the lips are thick and brutal, pure evil – they know how to spit. In this same photograph, the eyes are small and heavy-lidded, expressionless under very thick brows which have obviously been hand-touched; the calculated result makes him look ten years older, one ugly and most unpleasant character, the kind to avoid. Then, at what appears to have been the very same session, his white face stands out in blackness, the profile highlighted, looking out to the side while his ringed hands are clasped on a box that might well be an altar. He is also, to display the young boy in himself, seen in normal light, frolicking with a puppy: a shot for the mothers.

The amount of press photographs released during this time is quite staggering; a veritable deluge, it covers the world, showing Elvis as a saint, as a sinner, as a clean boy, as a beast that should not be let loose, as a dreamy romantic. The photographs are designed to appeal to every kind of fan, and to compliment the frequently bewildering collage of singing styles that young Elvis is offering to a pop-eyed world. He will never be bigger than he is during this period, and the photographs like the records whose style is almost imperceptibly changing are the first calculated refutation of his primitive image. The "mean" shots are quickly dropped.

By 1956 there are Elvis shirts, slacks, sweaters, bracelets, belts, ties, hats, T-shirts, dogs, dolls, greeting cards, bubble gum cards, pins, pens, pencils, buttons, pillows, combs,

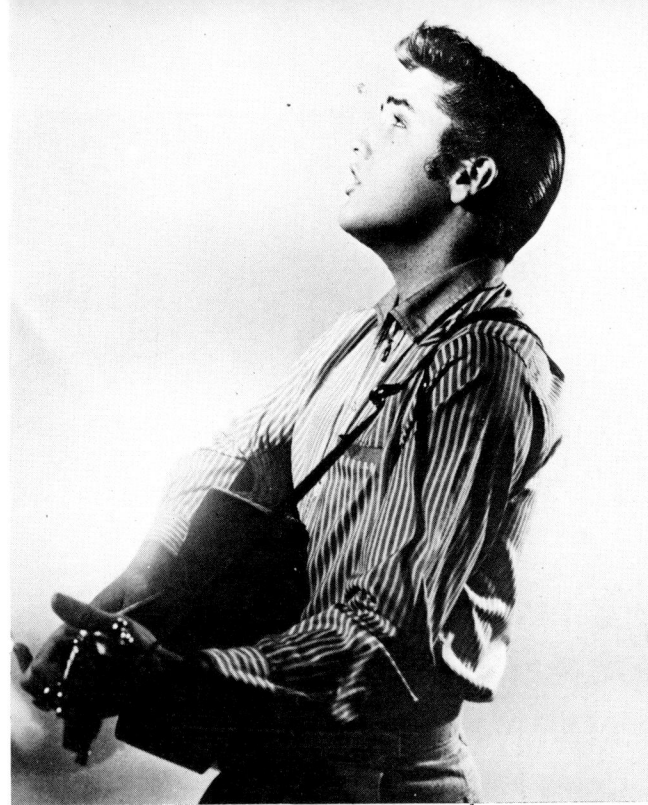

More publicity stills, 1956. Left: Four different faces from the same session. Right: a final "mean" shot.

hairbrushes, busts, bookends, guitars, colognes, lipsticks (Hound Dog Orange, Heartbreak Hotel Pink, Tutti Frutti Red), shoes, shirts, socks, underpants, belts, chains, handkerchiefs, wallets, fan clubs, gangs, sects, sundry other organizations and special photographs that light up in the dark – plus, of course, all the records. (But no tie-ups, of course, with booze or cigarettes.)

Elvis has a gold-leaf suit that cost $4,000 and gold slippers that cost a meagre $100. He has a whole stream of cadillacs – yellow, pink, blue and purple. He has ''dozens of teddy bears, a live Australian wallaby, a pair of burros, two monkeys named Jayhue and Jimboe, a three-wheeled Messerschmidt, thirty sports coats and forty sports shirts ('His clothes have to be seen in compatible colour to be believed'), a swimming pool, and a $100,000 mansion that glows blue-and-gold in the dark.'' The kid knows how to spend it.

It is obviously the best time of his life; he is out to enjoy himself. Colonel Parker is advertising him with elephants and midgets (The Elvis Presley *Midget* Fan Club) and he himself is doing his bit. To calm the hysteria at one particular performance, he quips, ''Thank you. You bring a lump to my bill fold.'' Then, in reply to critics who think he is obscene, he makes a remark that will fill young fans with glee and will become part of pop literature: ''They all think I'm a sex maniac. They're all frustrated old types, anyway. I'm just natural.'' Some time later, accused of signing his autograph on young ladys' breasts, he neatly skips out with: ''I've written on arms, legs, ankles – any place decent where people can take soap and wash it off. I don't want no daddy with a shotgun after me.'' He also bites the hand of a female interviewer, explaining blandly: ''I was only being friendly like a little puppy dog.'' And when asked by a woman journalist how he feels about girls who throw themselves at him, he gives her his heavy-lidded burn and says: ''I usually take them.'' Finally, when he is asked why he hasn't gotten married, he

comes up with the pure corn-cob reply: "Why buy a cow when you can get milk under the fence?"

No doubt about it: he's got it, he can use it, and he plays with it. He also gets into fights (but always in defence), has a few lawsuits thrown at him by girls claiming to have his child, and has a good time, driving motor bikes and fast cars, dating starlets and painting the town red: a young man in his heyday.

The fans are now spread world-wide and are voracious in pursuit of him. Some pray to his picture before going to bed, carve his name into their forearms with jack-knives, or riot in the streets of what once were staid cities; others get expelled from school for refusing to cut their hair (make no mistake, the crew-cut is *dead*), run away from home to keep vigil at Graceland, crawl through his windows, climb over his cars, steal the trees from his garden, walk away with his statues – and at least ten-thousand of them write him letters each week, in which they express their undying and most suicidal love.

He is now considered to be "morally insane", is described as "an inspiration for low IQ hoodlums" who "ought to be entertaining in the State Reformatory", the reason doubtless being that he is practising "his voodoo of frustration and defiance" and is therefore a "whirling dervish of sex". Consequently, some of his records are publicly incinerated, more live performances are banned, and when he gets on television they wipe sweat from their brows and try straightening him out for the masses – and results are ludicrous.

On the *Milton Berle Show* Elvis wears a tuxedo with lapels that resemble shark fins. He seems decidedly uncomfortable, keeps fingering his bow tie, and at one stage actually mumbles, as if it wasn't rehearsed, "It's not that often that I get to wear the . . . er . . . suit and tails." There are Roman columns behind him, the guitar seems out of place, but his singing gets the message across – there's no holding this boy. So he groans

Above: He sings "Hound Dog" to a hound dog on the Steve Allen Show. Facing page top: Andy Griffith, Imogene Coca, Steve Allen and Elvis (Tumbleweed) Presley. Bottom: Elvis with Milton Berle and Elvis with Tommy and Jimmy Dorsey, 1956.

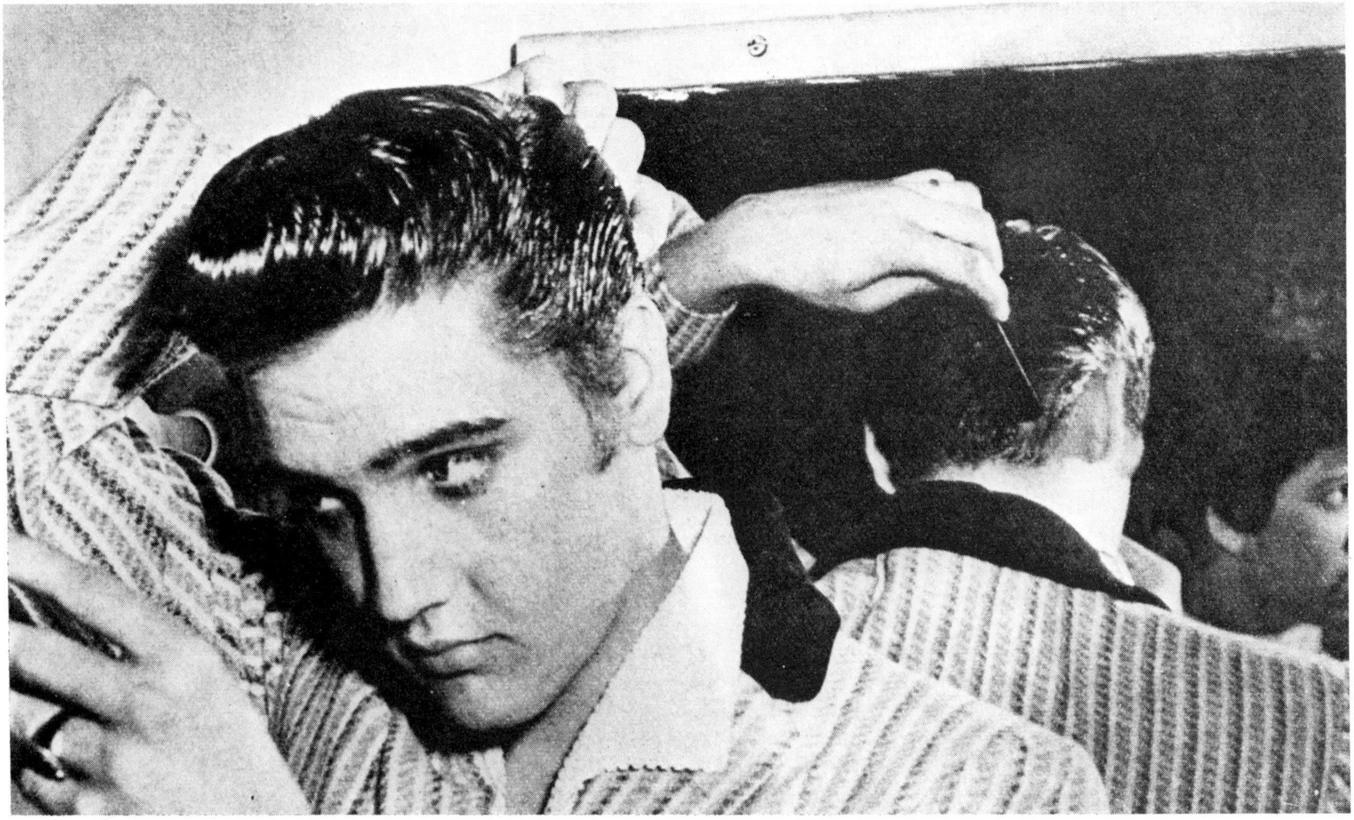

out *"I want you! I need you! I love you!"* and the girls in the audience start shrieking. This is just the beginning.

The *Steve Allen Show* is worse, pure insanity. With Steve Allen, Andy Griffith and a lady called Imogene Coca, he endures a thoroughly silly and humourless Western sketch based around the selling of a "Tonto Chocolate Bar". It is presumably a satire on the Louisiana Hayride, but it sinks fast under its yipee-aye-ohs. Elvis, known as Tumbleweed, is

submerged in the background and only comes forward on occasion to sing some abysmal lines. He wears a white sombrero and a black cowboy outfit, is handsome and otherwise lost. Then he changes into a tuxedo, they wheel on a droopy dog, and Elvis chants his song right in its face, before kissing its nose. He doesn't get to move much, but he sneaks in the odd shiver, and that just about wraps it up for the day. The show is a huge success.

On the *Ed Sullivan Show*, where he's told to stay subdued, he manages to be better: he insinuates. Against a dark, light-flecked background, his hair shining with laquer, he runs through "Don't be Cruel", starts to sway just a little – and is promptly cut off at the waist. He then introduces "Love Me Tender" – the title song of his first movie – and he sings it by plunging his fists in his pockets and rocking back slightly on his heels, his lip curling, just teasing. He is lazy, greasy, and he's Rudolph Valentino – sliding a hand down one thigh, shrugging his shoulders just for kicks, and very slyly mocking the sentiment of the song, sometimes rolling his eyeballs. The

girls go bananas, their shrieks shake the cameras, and Mr Sullivan is losing pounds as he stands in the wings. Later, Elvis Presley saunters back before the cameras to publicise his newest LP. His hands hang loose and limp, he sways dreamily from side to side, he cups one hand over an ear in imitation of Johnny Ray, and on the last line of "Love Me" – a long, drawn-out "OOOHH!" – he suddenly grabs hold of his head, shakes it vigorously and howls *"Love me!"* as if he's been knifed by a madman. It brings the house down.

But these television shows are a harbinger of things to come. As his records change, softening his approach, spreading over the whole spectrum of popular music in an attempt to corner all of the market, so he achieves the desired effect. As he comes on with the ballads, with the teardrops and perfume, he is, with his very sound instincts, preparing himself for what he will need when he gets to Hollywood – which, to be sure, is where he's heading. If he never leaves America (and as a performer he never does), the silver screen will carry him to foreign lands, make him a household word. He will be like Dean Martin, Bing Crosby, Frank Sinatra: he will aim for an Oscar and retire, a respectable man. Rock 'n' roll is a fad, has no hope in Hell of lasting, and if you want to survive you get out while the going is good. In this, as in many other myths, Hollywood is the answer.

His debut is one of the most entertaining camp performances of all time. Originally called *The Reno Brothers*, the movie is

Below: Elvis signs up with producer Hal Wallis to a killing seven-year contract. He'll seldom look so happy for some time after. Opposite page: Love Me Tender *(1957).*

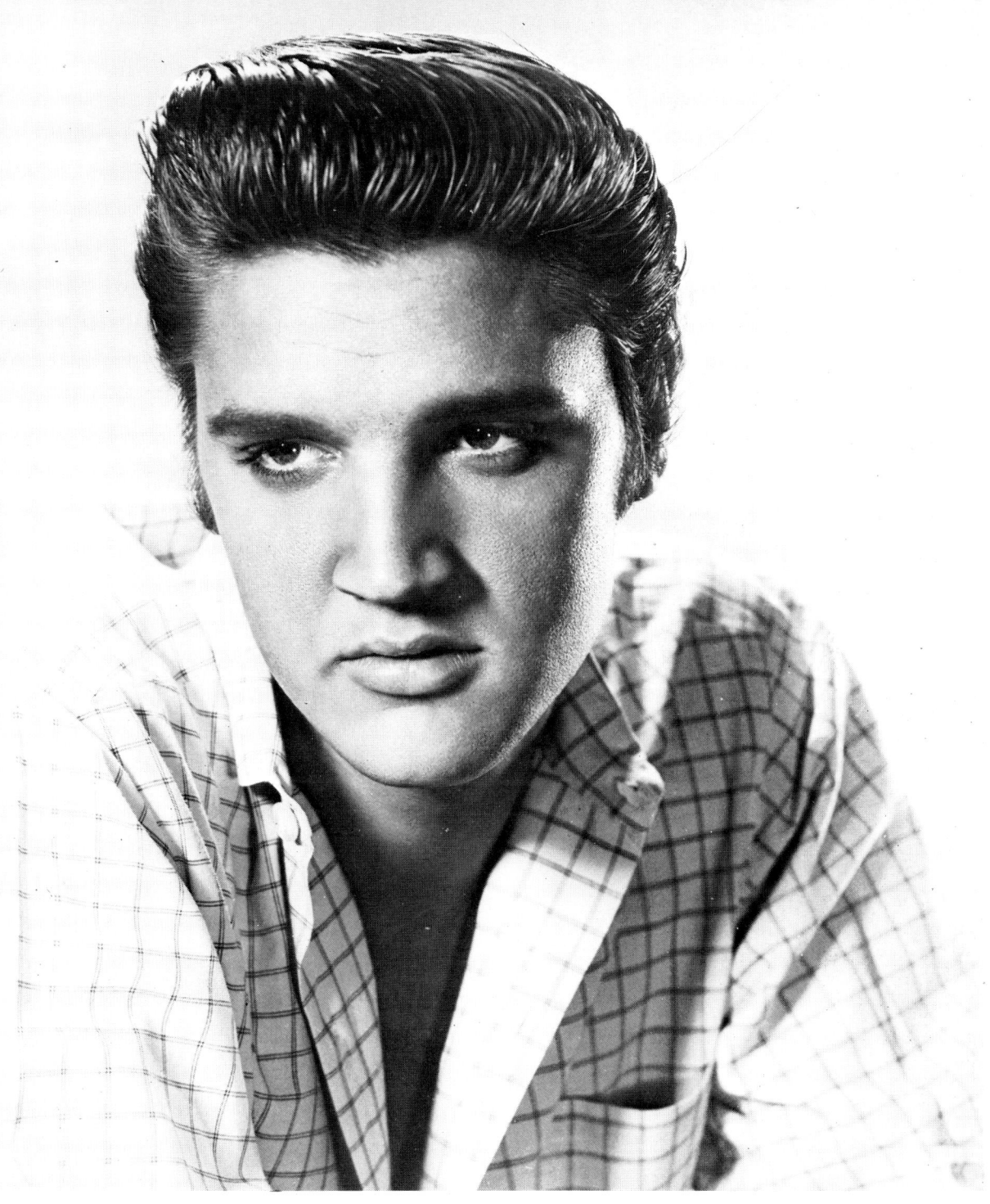

retitled *Love Me Tender* (1957) to cash in on the kid's latest hit. (There aren't supposed to be songs, but when they realise what they're dealing with, they promptly slip four of them in.) Very much a ''B'' grade look at the American Civil War, it features young Elvis Presley as an innocent ploughboy who falls in love with, and then marries, his brother's girlfriend. The brother, who was thought to have been killed by the damned Yanks, returns to try and start life again – which makes for embarrassment. The rest of the film is a confused, grainy sortie into shootin', lootin' and general mayhem, during which the greasy kid performs four country songs and manages to die, after much heroic lingering, with his own ghost singing hazily about him – a fantastic finale. As for Presley's performance, it is passionately sincere, if wildly off-key. Fans will later complain about the ''almost childlike persistence

of the other stars in trying to 'better' Elvis's lines'' – but the other stars show more sense: they simply sleep-walk around him.

The film does, however, prove that Elvis has real presence, a most natural gift for projection, an animal vigour. The songs are disappointing to those expecting hard rock, but are the only kind possible in a period piece. Later they will stand up as undefiled hillbilly boppers, sung crisply and with unerring instinct; but at the time they are forgotten as throwaways, last minute additions. Still, the kid quivers and shakes like a jelly, legs bending and rolling in spasms, the guitar pointing skyward. It's the very first time that non-Americans have seen him, and what they see doesn't disappoint them: he is dreamy, sublime, the greatest thing since James Dean. And who wouldn't weep at such a death scene?

The film *Love Me Tender* enamours no critics, makes a fortune at the box office, and causes more riots in the streets. After being informed that his "dramatic contribution is not a great deal more impressive than that of one of the slavering nags", young Elvis, undeterred, tries another. *Loving You* (1957) is more ambitious (technicolour, no less) and its main theme is simply the rise to success of a young man much like Elvis himself. As a film it's much better than it is ever given credit for – a woefully sentimentalised, but otherwise quite accurate, examination of the rise of a pop star in the American south-west.

Elvis plays Deke Rivers, a small-town boy with a natural ability for putting over his own kind of music, specifically rock 'n' roll. He is picked up by a beautifully, calculating press agent, who sees in him the chance to revive the flagging

Love Me Tender *(1957). A 20th Century-Fox release,
produced by David Weisbart, directed by Robert D. Webb,
and co-starring Richard Egan, Debra Paget, William
Campbell, Neville Brand and Mildred Dunnock. The film ran
for eighty-nine minutes which was approximately eighty
minutes too long (Elvis sang the other nine minutes). A
confused, grainy sortie into shootin', lootin' and general
mayhem, it gave Elvis four country songs ("Love Me Tender",
"Let Me", "Poor Boy" and "We're Gonna Move") and
allowed him finally to die, after much heroic lingering. A
critical disaster, it made a mint at the box office and turned
Elvis into the new golden boy of Hollywood. Above: Elvis
sings to his family on the porch, including Debra Paget (as
his wife) and Mildred Dunnock (as his mother). Opposite:
Colonel Parker, Elvis, William Campbell and El's cousin,
Gene Smith, on the set.*

Left: Another still from Love Me Tender. *Below left: A rare shot of Elvis recording the film's soundtrack, with J. D. Fontana on drums. The guitar pose was taken during filming, but not actually filmed. Meanwhile, other work (and play) continued. Bottom: Elvis running through a song with the Jordanaires. Opposite: various "candid" shots of our boy on the loose. The one at bottom right is a classic example of young lovers in the fifties, complete with Eisenhower clothing and transport.*

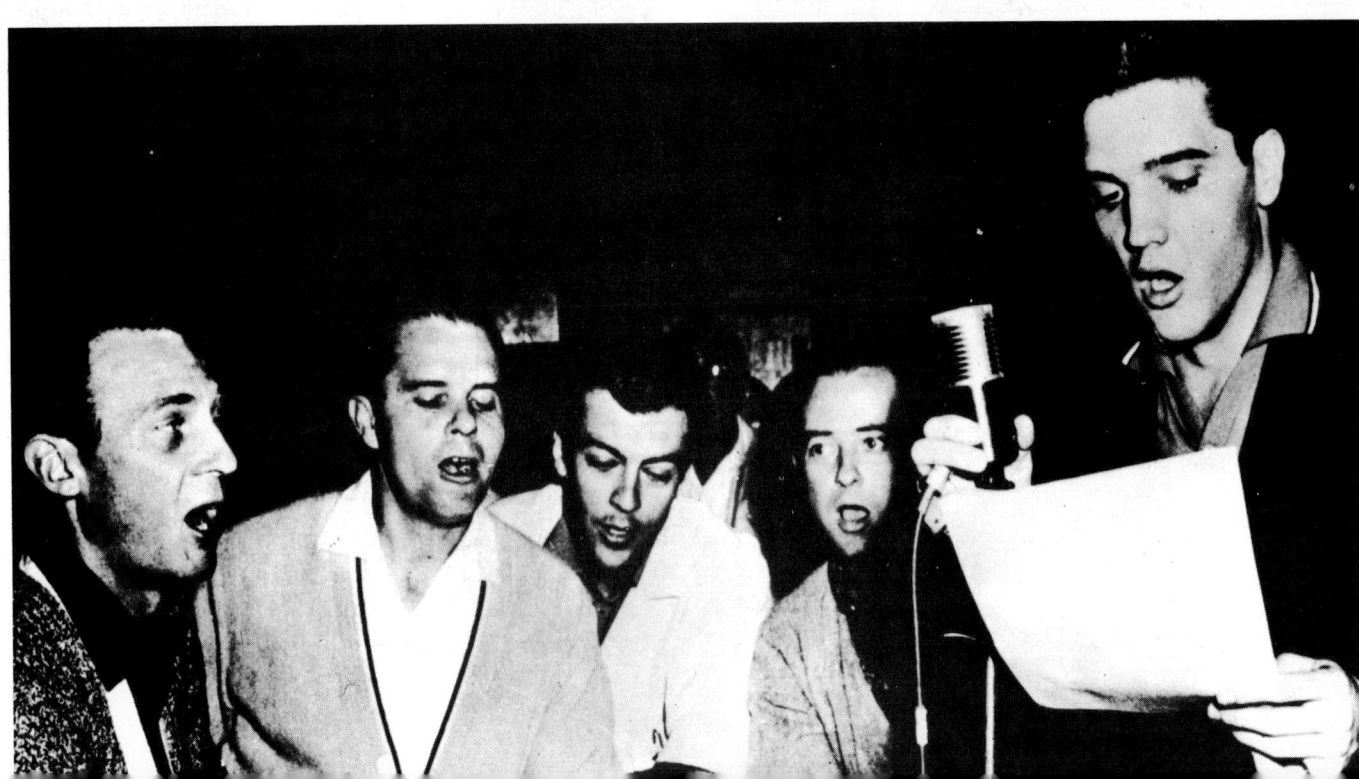

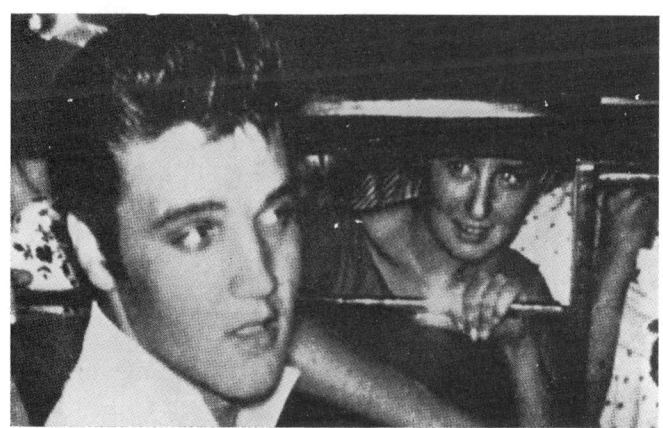

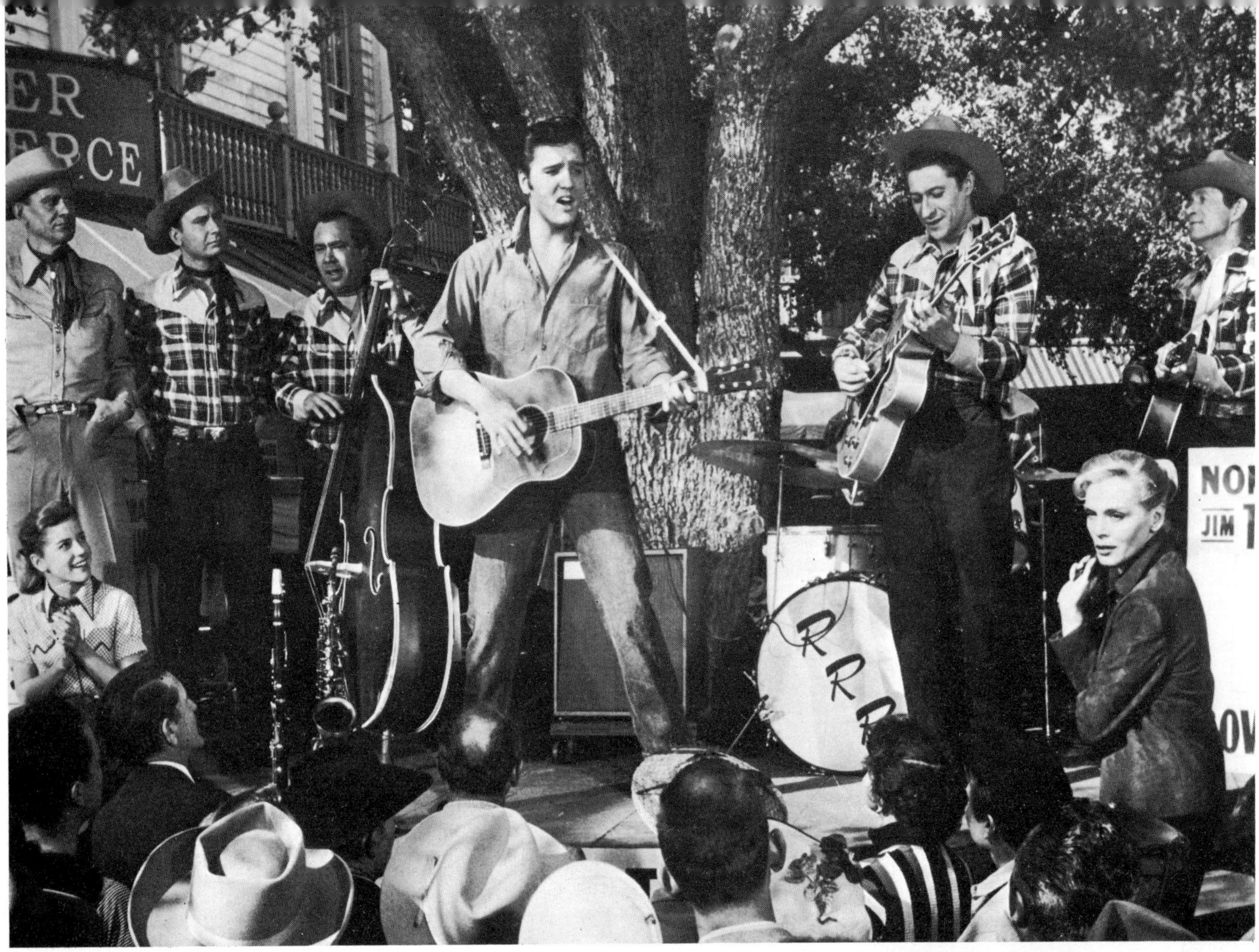

Loving You (1957). A Paramount Picture, produced by Hal Wallis, directed by Hal Kanter, and co-starring Lizabeth Scott, Wendell Cory and Dolores Hart. Critically underrated at the time of its release, it is now considered by some to be one of the best of the genre. A reasonably accurate examination of the rise of a young pop star in the American southwest, it unconsciously mirrors Presley's own changing career – from blue-denimmed rough-neck (above) to phosphorescent dream-image (opposite page). The film used lots of shadow and romantic back-lighting to emphasise the "mythic" qualities of its star; it also smoothed out his face, painted his lips and eyes, and offered him up as an aphrodisiac to the needy. Actually seen playing with Elvis in the movie are Bill Black (bass) and Scotty Moore (guitar). Shortly after this these old friends would go their separate ways.

fortunes of her ex-husband's simple country band. She takes the kid on tour with them, but pretty soon he's much bigger than the band he's supposed to be aiding. This leads to jealousy and resentment on the part of her ex-husband, who views the kid as a threat not only to his own career but to the love that he still has for his woman. On top of which (a most cunning device) the kid is sensitive, lonely, bewildered by his success, and unaware of how he is being used: instant audience sympathy.

The film uses this simple theme as a basic prop around which to hang some good production numbers; it presents the songs well and it's the only one in his career that seems to have a firm grip on what he is. It also manages, for the first and the last time, to present Elvis as he is on the stage . . . well, not quite, but close enough. And finally, most certainly, it

marks the beginning of the tidying up of Mr Presley: the smooth-faced, unreal man.

It takes Presley's own history – his humble background, his rise to fame – and neatly ties it to the current craze for tortured teen heroes. He is therefore shown singing and fighting and quietly brooding, talking often in a whisper, face dramatically shadowed, a real blue-denimmed child of the fifties, struggling through. It also emphasises, since it is currently fashionable, that he really doesn't give a damn for his success: he just wants some lovin'.

Its technique is lascivious.

He is first seen in a very natural light: wearing denims, looking grubby and unsure of himself. The first song is performed while he's still wearing these clothes, standing on the back of an open flat-top truck, legs spread and a guitar in his hands – the quintessential Elvis pose. The song is the first version of "Got a Lot of Livin' to Do", and he starts it looking nervous, glancing cagily around him, holding on to his guitar as if for comfort, not really involved. Then, as he starts to get into his bit, he rocks back on his heels, lets his left hand hang limp, and simultaneously shakes his left leg – a modest, witholding version. He finishes by quivering, swinging his right arm and then breaking a string on his guitar: a foretaste of the future.

As the film progresses, as Deke becomes more popular, we see him performing on the truck and in marquees and getting just a little wilder each time. He does "Hot Dog" and "Party", and though he's still in blue jeans, he is more the Elvis we know, swinging arms, shaking legs. One of his favourite tricks is to rock back on his heels, let the spasms jolt up through his body as if through his feet: he's not really moving, he's just quivering all over; he's like something plugged in to a power point, being jolted to death. And indeed, since the

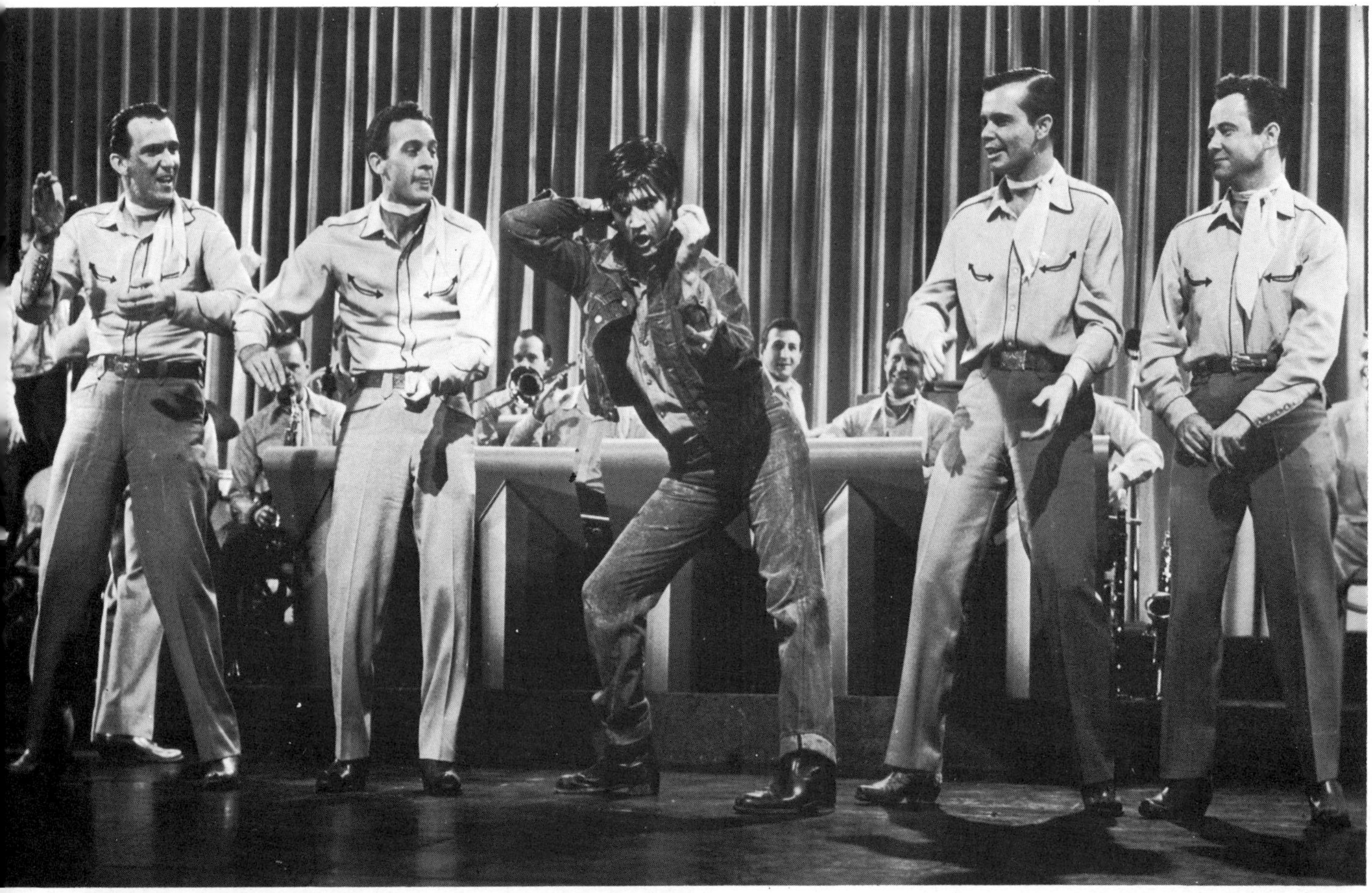
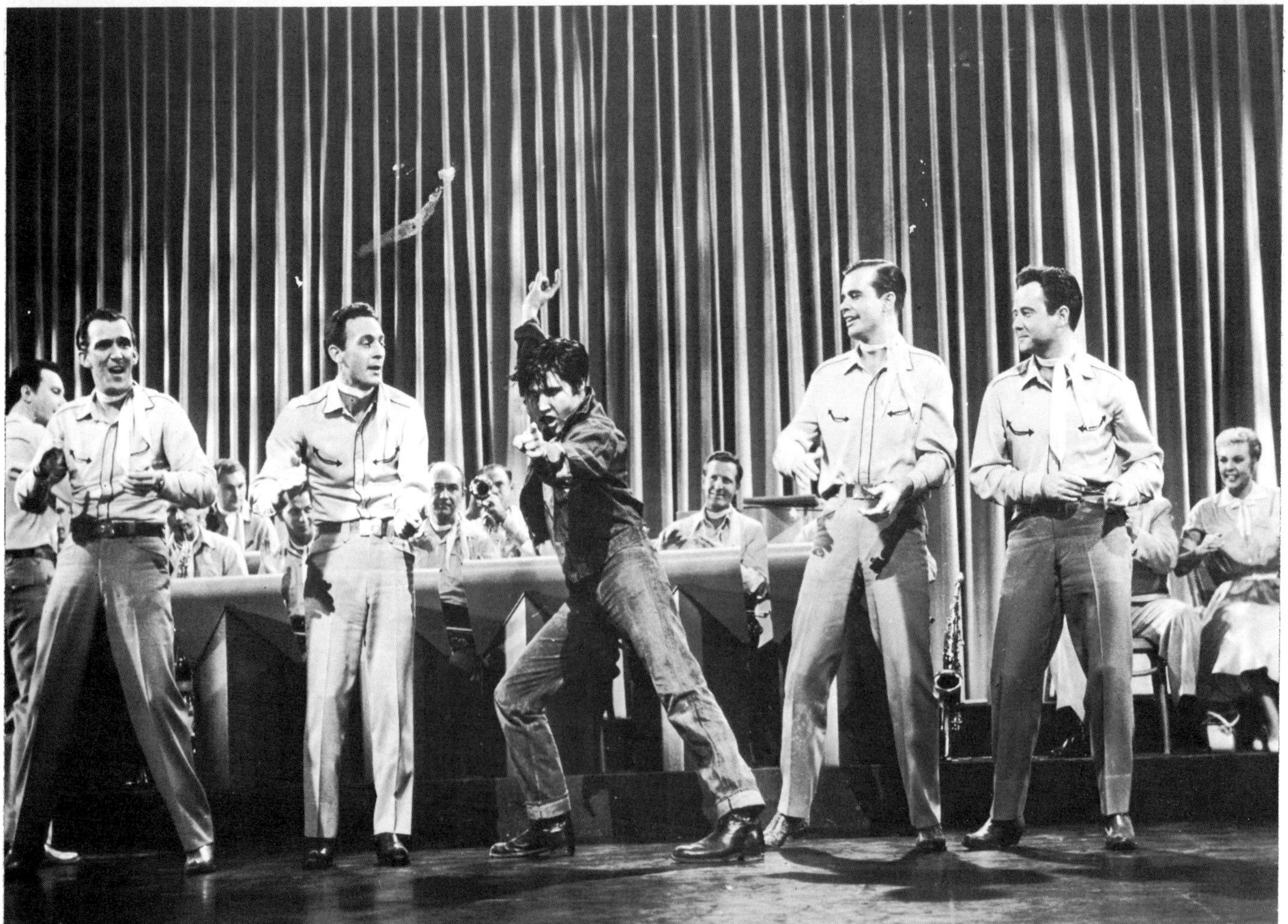

film always places him before an audience, the shrieking on the screen is often indistinguishable from the shrieking of those in the cinemas. Much craftier you can't get.

The film now outlines the way in which pop stars are processed. Deke Rivers grows more famous, sings ballads and softer rock, dresses flashily and enters real theatres where the decor is abstract. "Teddy Bear" is a rock song sung almost in a whisper – and the singer is the kind you don't find in the streets. His hair is stark black and shiny, his eyes are inked in, he wears tight red trousers with white seams down the sides, and his shirt is phosphorescent, a light-reflecting silk, all white but for the collar, shoulders and cuffs, which are red with white flowers·and fancy patterns. The stage behind him is dreamy, a veritable rainbow of colours, and the shadows fall crimson and mauve on his smooth, suntanned face. He doesn't play the guitar, he just holds it at an angle; and he represents a creature so wonderful as to be beyond the realms of mere mortality: a highly glamorised, perfect male.

Prior to this he has tackled "Lonesome Cowboy", and though he hasn't yet reached the very heights of golden glitter, the presentation is just as dream-like. He wears a checkered shirt and necktie, never plays his guitar, and is seen in a spotlight that cuts through the darkness to highlight his deep, long-lashed eyes, his hair shining like cut glass. Then he spreads wide his legs, turns slightly to the side, shows a clenched fist and swings one strong arm: he is no man to mix with.

This film does, in fact, use lots of shadow to emphasise

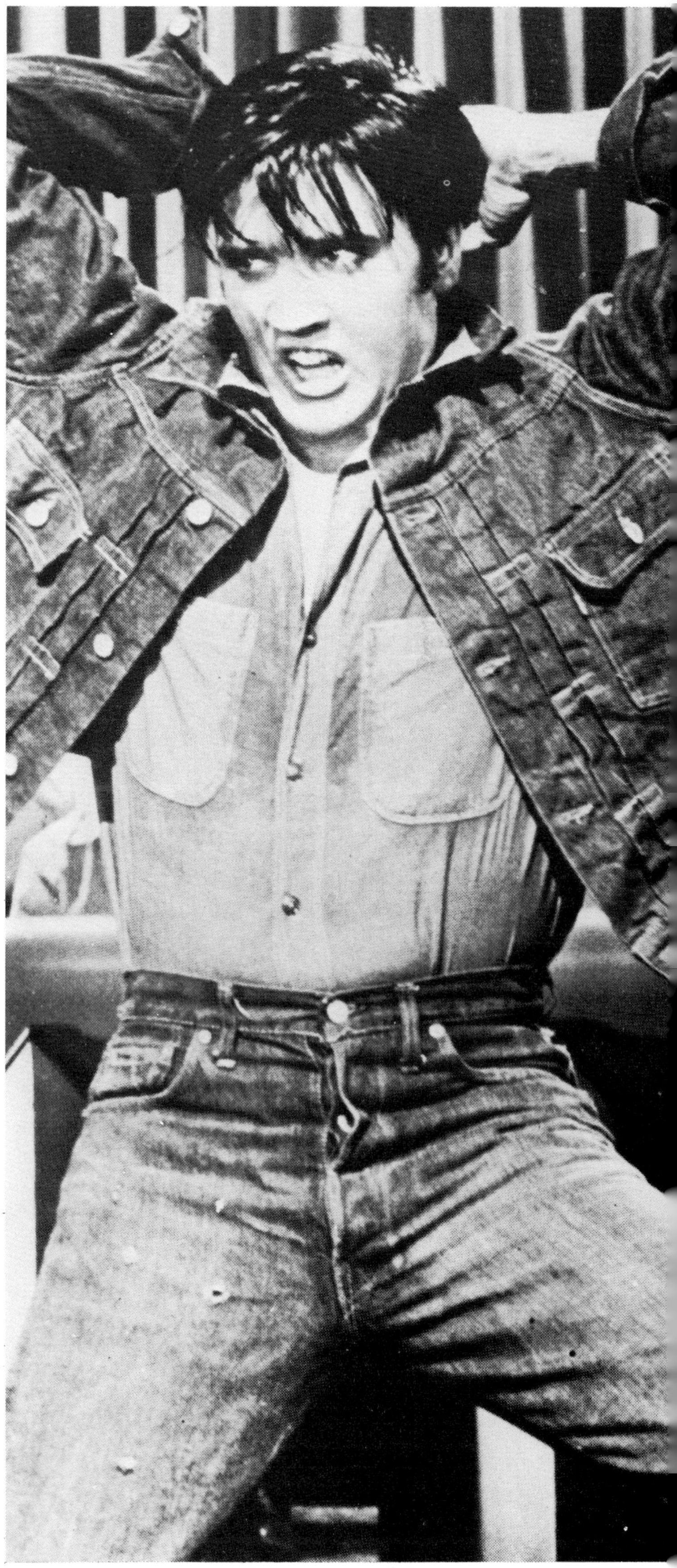

Elvis in action in Loving You, *singing "Got A Lot O' Livin' To Do". He will never be as wild as this again.*

Opposite: A dramatically shadowed Elvis in Loving You.
Above: Highly stylised publicity stills from the film.

the mythic qualities of its star. It also smooths out his face, paints his lips and his eyes, and offers him up as a meal for the hungry dreamer. (When the kid has a fight it is not his own fault: he is set upon; when he loves it is definitely without genitals: his kiss is a climax.) If the film is not great art it is still an accurate representation of the emotional climate of its

times, one of the very best of the "teen" movies. And Presley's performance, though no confident earth-shaker, is perfectly matched to its material and remains quite undated. In fact were he not a pop singer, maybe he would receive more serious attention than he is going to get. The pity here is that his personality is such that it can't be ignored by the

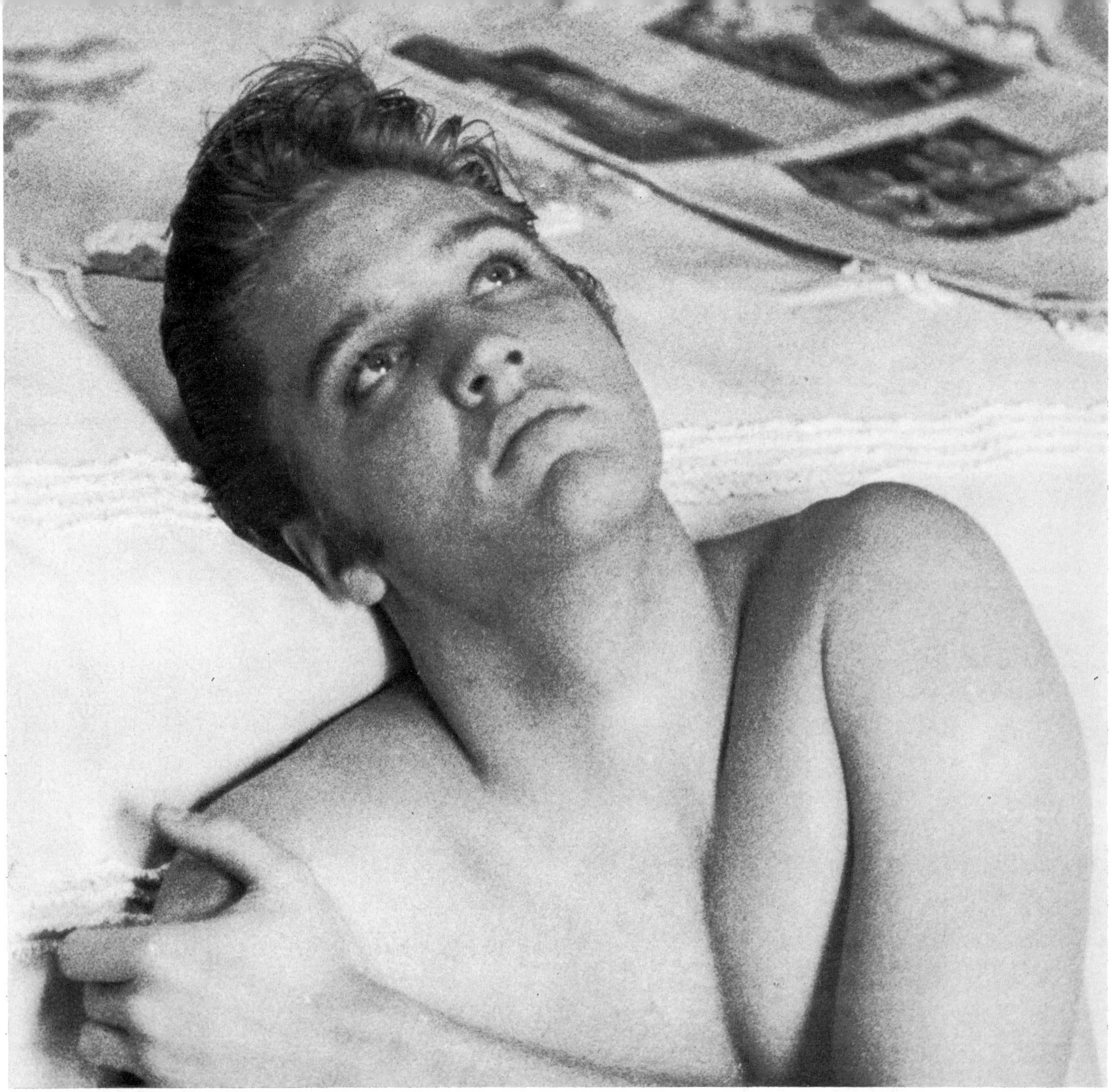

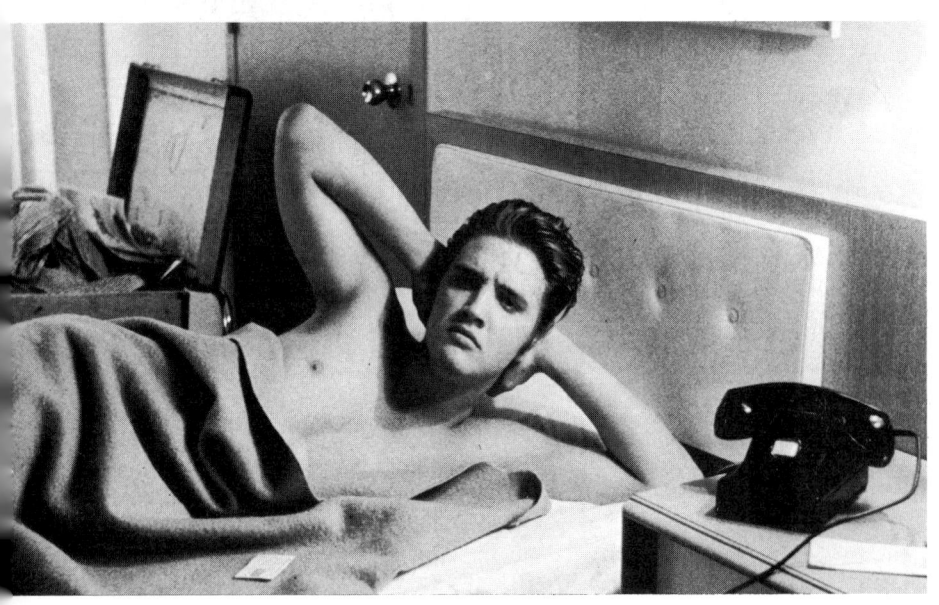

critics: and after all it is just a rock movie.

But for rock 'n' roll movies, it is very good indeed, showing up our prime performer as we most prefer him: gyrating his groin, swinging his arms, pumping out his hips, shaking all over, and dragging his bent left leg along a stage ramp like a cripple reaching out for the sacred cup: pure untrammelled showmanship.

Naturally, the film is a smash, causing riots and huge queues. It is condemned from the pulpit, often viewed by the police, and even banned in some backwater counties where they think it's a devil's tool. Meanwhile the soundtrack is rushed out and snapped up, while some singles taken off the LP thunder straight up the charts. The movie has proven that Elvis can hold the screen, but in doing so it changes his direction, sweetens his image. He is now in the arena of the great family audience and certain items have to be considered – such as children and grandmas. It won't happen abruptly – the changes will be subtle – but the changes must definitely come and are already prepared.

Jailhouse Rock (1958) has become the epitome of "punk." movies – a nice, greasy film about arrogance and deceit, about ambition and greed, about a slick sonofabitch who claws his way to the top and leaves his footprints on the faces of his old friends . . . but it ain't what it seems. It shines the spotlight on life's most human vermin, it is cynical and brittle and very funny. But within all the toughness, the comic-book realism, there beats the soft heart of a sentimental hack.

The film is made at the height of Elvis's fame, when he is still viewed as a revolting teenage fad, the first of the tough, punk rock singers. The producers, therefore, aren't about to sink the ship: they want to sell him to the fans, to all the kids

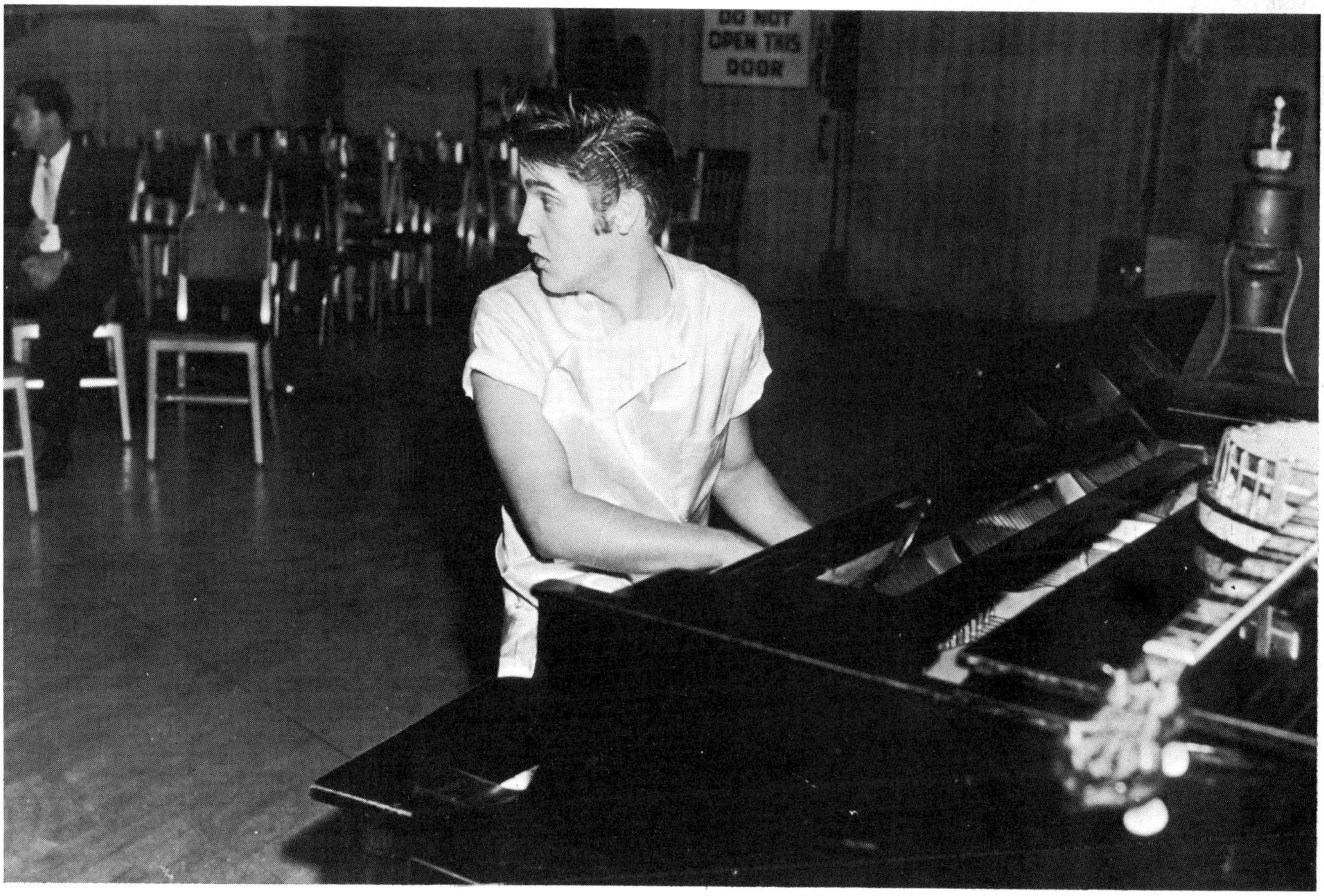

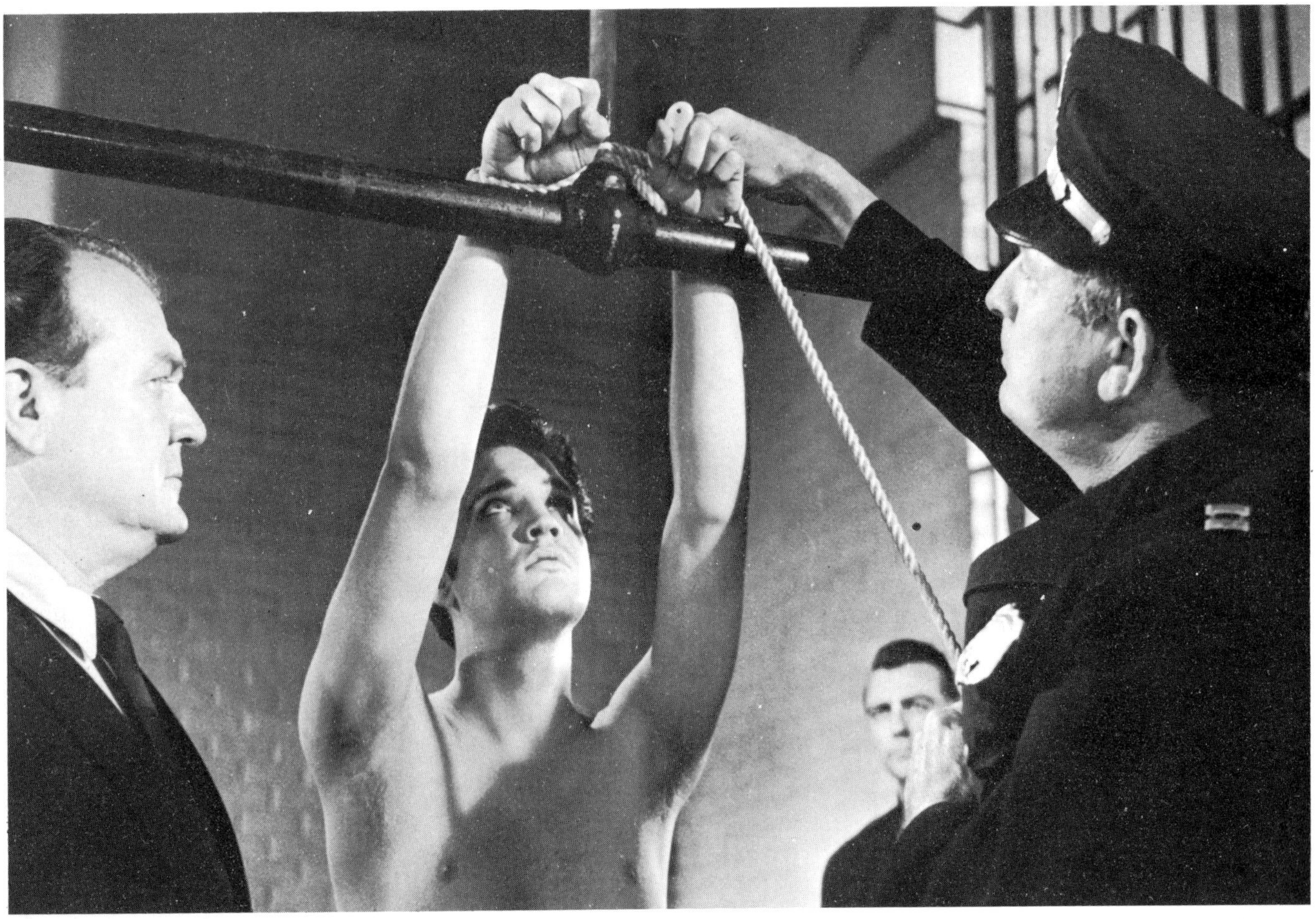

Jailhouse Rock *(1958). An M-G-M Picture, produced by Pandro S. Berman, directed by Richard Thorpe, and co-starring Mickey Shaughnessy, Judy Tyler, Jennifer Holden and Dean Jones. Disdained by the critics and condemned from the pulpit, this highly entertaining look at a hoodlum pop star has since become something of a cult movie. Above: Our hero is stripped to the waist and brutally flogged. Left: He is corrupted by worldly Mickey Shaughnessy. Opposite page: Three classic examples of this new, and thrillingly nasty, Elvis. Top left: He tackles Judy Tyler, growling "That ain't tactics, honey, that's jest the beast in me." Top right: he sneeringly offers popcorn to a dumb blonde (Jennifer Holden). Bottom: He is filmed through the legs of a stripper with his gaze very cunningly aligned. Overleaf is the flamboyant "Jailhouse Rock" dance routine.*

who like this snake, but they also want to broaden the scope, to add tears to the tantrums. So they have him real mean, a real fireball and sexy, and they lay out the shock effects nicely before pouring the cream. Thus, he is miraculously brought back to basic decency – to the real, softer *him* and in doing so they manage to weight the scale at both ends – and destroy an almost perfect piece of *kitsch*.

Once more the simple theme is the rise from rags to riches, but this time the gimmick, the irresistible novelty, is that the kid is an unrepentant ex-con. At first he's a nice boy – just a little bit wild – but then, when he gallantly defends a lady's honour, he accidentally kills her tormentor and gets sent up the river.

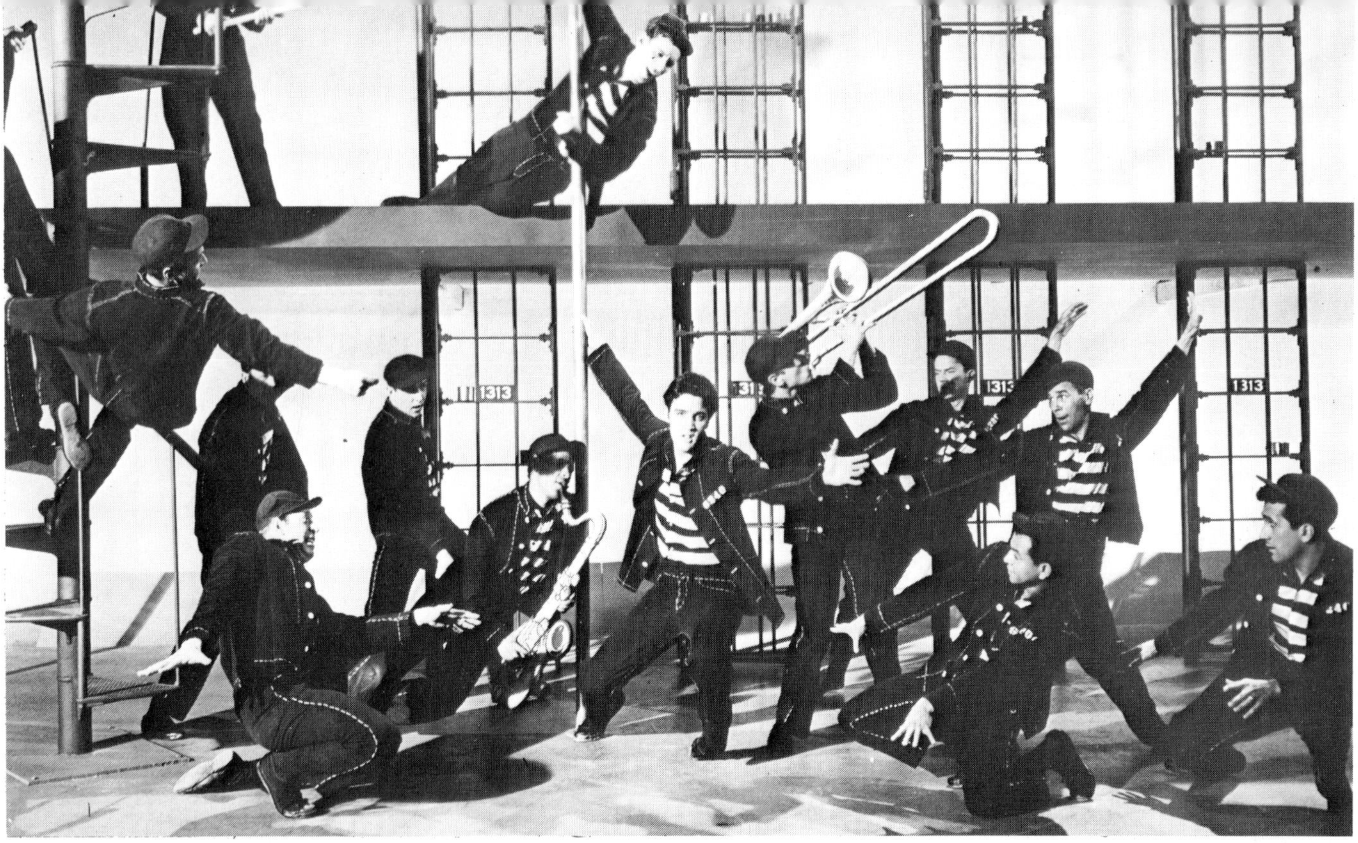

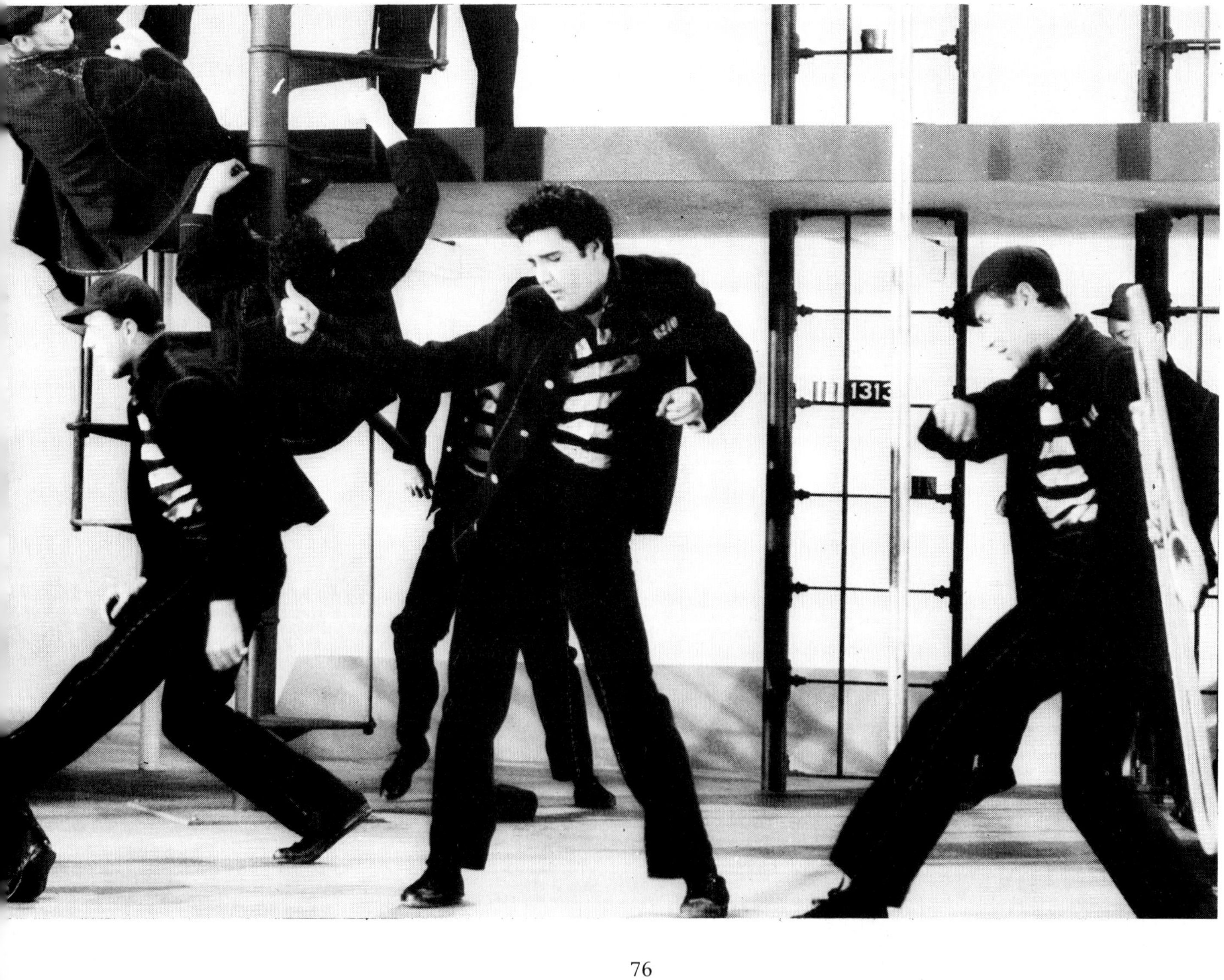

The injustice of this makes him cynical. And once inside the Big House, he learns the ways of the wicked world, has his lovely locks shorn (the biggest gimmick in the movie) and gets blamed for a riot he didn't start. He is then stripped to the waist and quite thrillingly flogged (the second biggest gimmick in the movie) and goes back to his cell gritting perfect teeth.

He has now been corrupted by the corruption of the world and he'll go out for all he can get: his soft heart has been hardened. Remarkably, he learns to play the guitar; even more remarkably, he manages to make an appearance on a show that is televised from the prison. And to stretch credibility even farther, his cell mate (Mickey Shaughnessy) gets his signature on a contract prior to his discharge from the brig.

"Watch out for the teeth, sonny", he's advised when he departs. "It's a jungle."

So the kid sneers and leaves, his eyes cold as ballbearings, and meets up with a lovely press agent who starts turning him into a star while she fights off his uncouth advances. "I like the way you swing a guitar", she says lasciviously – and then turns all puritanical when the brute lifts his huge paws. "Don't try your cheap tactics on me!" she primly tells him. To which he replies, with his lip curling superbly: "That ain't tactics, honey. That's jest the beast in me."

He gets famous as a singer, buys himself some fancy gear, and starts knocking off the birds right and left because his agent rejected him. He then goes to Hollywood, has parties by the pool, buys some dogs and treats them better than the humans, most of whom he just tramples on. He spits on his friends, almost cuts his true love's heart out, and says to Mickey Shaughnessy, who now walks all the dogs: "You're just gettin' bitter, old buddy." For which there is good cause.

Towards the end of the film, he's attacked by his dog-walker because he's been so mean to his true love, whom the

Above: Jailhouse Rock's arrogant Elvis explodes into action.
Opposite: The Big "E" with his Harley Davidson on the
M-G-M lot between takes on the Jailhouse Rock film.

dog-walker also loves. He loses his voice (sighs of dread in the cinema) and it looks like he'll never get it back – thus he instantly repents. As is true in real life, repentance always works the miracle, and this film doesn't argue with that. Elvis takes off his bandages, looks at his true love, almost weeps and then opens his golden throat – the violins come rushing in.

Hardly a synopsis to suggest a softening process, but the soft soap is definitely there. The film will become most famous

for Elvis's performance, which is even more entertaining than Mickey Shaughnessy's. He is arrogant and sexy, violent and sarcastic, and he delivers his lines with a soft icy edge that enlivens them more than they're worth. It is true of this film that until the very last reel he doesn't even bother trying to woo his audience; he stifles his natural charm. But the film is rigged to make each nasty trick seem the product of some deep inner hurt: he is merely defensive.

What really comes out in the film – and it's a harbinger of the future – is the degree to which Presley has been stylised. The most celebrated production number is the "Jailhouse Rock" sequence, which is big, bold, brassy and as slick as they come. But Elvis's free-wheeling style, which *Loving You* managed to catch, is here tightly controlled and drastically subordinated to an immaculately choreographed routine which entertains without exciting. Elvis moves like a snake, is professionally beyond criticism, but one feels that any male chorus dancer could have done the thing for him. What is missing is the element of violence, of visual surprise; what is left is a competent but standardised Hollywood gang show.

There are two other rock songs in the film, but neither is presented well. He sings "Baby I Don't Care" by the side of the swimming pool and his gestures, which are supposed to be sophisticated, are merely grotesque. The second rock song – his classic version of "Treat Me Nice" – is presented as a studio recording, which necessarily limits him. He occasionally snaps his fingers, sways his hips, shakes a leg, but for the most part he is subdued, a mere Hollywood swinger. The last song in the film, which should have been a real raver, is a ballad which he offers with glistening eyes. And it is this calculated run-

down – from hard rock to soft ballads – which will guide the song sequence of his next movie: he will leave them in tears.

He is now a long way from Memphis, even farther from Tupelo, is ensconced in the whirlwind and glitter of Holywood, cutting records in Culver City, at the M-G-M studios, and hiding out with his "ol' boys" in the biggest hotels, hiring movies, drinking Cokes, and sneaking out in the morning hours surrounded by bodyguards, with his "mafia" and yes-men, to try to have a little fun without the fans swarming down on his mortal flesh. Sometimes he visits Graceland, his blue-and-gold glowing mansion, and he still makes live appearances between film commitments. But now the army calls him and he wants to do it right, so he makes one last movie which will be his best – though it will show also with a depressing skill that the rocking Elvis Presley is about to be buried in favour of a more general approach: he will finally be smooth.

Within its narrow limitations, *King Creole* (1958) is a film almost perfectly realised and executed. Shot in black and white on

location in New Orleans, it is directed by Michael Curtiz with a great eye for detail and shows his ability to get the best from his actors. The supporting cast is any young actor's dream: the superb Walter Matthau, Carolyn Jones and Dean Jagger, not to mention the underrated Vic Morrow as the local flick knife. It is further enhanced by having Presley's finest soundtrack collection – though the treatment of these songs will be the most disappointing aspect of the production.

The film opens with some beautifully lit shots of the desolate, rain-damp, early morning New Orleans' streets. A black woman trundles her cart along, singing out to advertise her wares. Elvis, playing a kid named Danny Fisher, comes out on his latticed balcony and sings ''Crawfish'', an excellent pastiche Creole song. He leans on the railing, tucks in his shirt,

King Creole *(1958). A Paramount Picture, produced by Hal Wallis and directed by Michael Curtiz. Labelled by some critics as the ''Blackboard Jungle'' of pop, it was Elvis' most violent film – and certainly his best. The supporting cast was any young actor's dream, and included the superb Walter Matthue, Carolyn Jones and Dean Jagger, with Vic Morrow as the only delinquent to equal Elvis. Elvis obviously learnt a lot from these professionals; his performance was excellent. Unfortunately a major mistake lay in reuniting him with Dolores Hart, surely one of the most saccharine girls in the film business. His love affair with her was only matched by the insipid treatment of some otherwise wonderful songs. These pages show the ''smooth'' Elvis performing his numbers. From left to right: ''Trouble'', ''New Orleans'' and ''As Long As I Have You''. Overleaf: Elvis mixes with some bad company – with the exception of the lovely Lilliane Montevecchi.*

and sways his hips ever so gently: a smooth, sinuous performance.

The kid is basically decent, but he's dissatisfied and rebellious, and considers his father a weakling. He isn't getting on at school, is not particularly interested in anything, and cleans up in a local night club to bring in needed money. This morning, when he goes to the club to clean up, he meets a pair of local hoods and an alcoholic moll (Carolyn Jones). They want some music, but it isn't available, so they insist that the kid sing a song. He does ''Steadfast, Loyal and True'' – his school's Alma Mater – his hands folded primly in front of him, his voice nervous but true. When he's finished, one of the hoods assaults Carolyn before turning on Elvis himself. Elvis smashes two bottles on a table and seems to know how to use them.

''You're a pretty fancy performer, kid'', says one of the hoods.

"Now you know what I do for an encore", Elvis replies.

The kid now has to go to school, so he shares a taxi with Miss Jones, and when they get there, she insists that he kiss her. The other kids see this, start hooting and hollering, and Elvis loses his temper and takes a poke at one. For this minor offence, he's told that he won't be graduating, which is news that could cripple his father. Then, on the way home, through the dark-shadowed alleys, he's waylaid by Vic Morrow and his gang. Vic pulls out his flick knife, but is grabbed by the throat and slammed violently into the nearest wall. So impressed is the hooligan by this brilliant display that he promptly invites Elvis to join his gang. Elvis refuses.

"Good boy," murmurs Vic, closing up his glittering knife. "Fights real dirty."

When Elvis arrives home he breaks the bad news to his father (the excellent Dean Jagger) and this causes yet another row between them. Elvis, disgusted, stomps out of the house and decides to join Vic's gang after all. The idea, would you believe, is that Elvis sing in a store to distract the staff and let the boys knock off some goodies. This they do, in a very amusing scene, while Elvis strums his guitar and croons "Lover Doll", a modest but catchy ballad. Then Elvis makes a date with a cute salesgirl witness, and he gets the hell out of the store.

That night, in the Blue Shade, Elvis speaks to the boozing lady, who is accompanied by the dreaded Maxie Fields (Walter Matthue), the crooked owner of this colourful den. Walter orders him to sing, so the kid gets right up there,

looks real mean and evil, and let's rip with one of his all-time classic numbers: *"If you're lookin' for trouble/You've come to the right place/If you're lookin' for trouble/Just look right in ma face . . ."* The song is an intriguing mixture of blues, jazz and rock, and it's raw vocal treatment is superb. The visual presentation is smooth rather than aggressive – a finger-snapping, hand-waving performance far removed from real rock. And it encourages the owner of a rival club to offer Elvis a job as a singer. This he does *not* refuse.

For his try-out performance at the King Creole club he does a hand-clapping "Dixieland Rock". It's a pure rock song with a Dixieland backing, and though the vocal is superb, the visual presentation is once more pinioned on the altar of a "sophisticated" approach, more suitable to Hollywood than to rock fans. Apart from shaking his head and snappily clapping his hands, he doesn't really do all that much. But he is, of course, a huge success.

The kid is now involved with Dolores Hart, who is virginal, and with Carolyn Jones, who is not. ("That's a pretty piece of material", he says of Carolyn's dress. "You ought to have a dress made out of it some day.") In between these minor romps he sings a ballad, "Young Dreams", and a superb gutter blues, "New Orleans". In both of these numbers the lighting is excellent, but the presentation is woefully stifled. He sings the ballad in a chair, snapping fingers, kicking legs, and otherwise looking quite trapped. Then, on the blues number, he's smooth and sinuous, but only his hands really move. It is, however, the best number in the movie, and the recorded

version is really quite remarkable: a stuttering, half-talking, and frequently howled piece of pure gold.

We are now only half-way through the film and the last rock song is sung. It's called "King Creole" and Presley's vocal is excellent, but he sings it without moving much. The legs are epileptic, the left hand hangs limp, but basically it's a static performance, nicely lit and well-regulated. And for the second half of the film there'll be no rock at all – we are now being prepared for the future.

Elvis is drawing all the crowds away from the wicked Walter Matthue's club, which doesn't please Walter at all. He thus employs Vic Morrow to involve the kid in a crime, which he can then hold over his head like a noose. Elvis's father has taken a job in a local pharmacy where he is constantly humiliated by the manager. Knowing that Elvis is much disturbed by this, Vic suggests that they beat up the manager, and Elvis agrees. Unfortunately they beat up his father instead – which leaves Elvis open to Walter's blackmail. Elvis is given no alternative but to sign up with Walter and move away from the King Creole club. During his farewell performance he sings "Don't Ask Me Why", and then gives a sad speech and disappears. He now works for Walter.

The rest of the film is a very fast-paced, if somewhat melodramatic, sequence of events. The kid's father goes to Walter to plead for the release of his boy and is informed that his son led his own attackers. This breaks him up, and Elvis, quite shocked, brutally beats Walter around his own flat. Walter then orders Vic to carve the kid up, which Vic manages to do before Elvis kills him. The wounded Elvis, his left arm pouring blood, staggers back to his father's front door, where he is promptly rejected. He staggers away, eventually faints

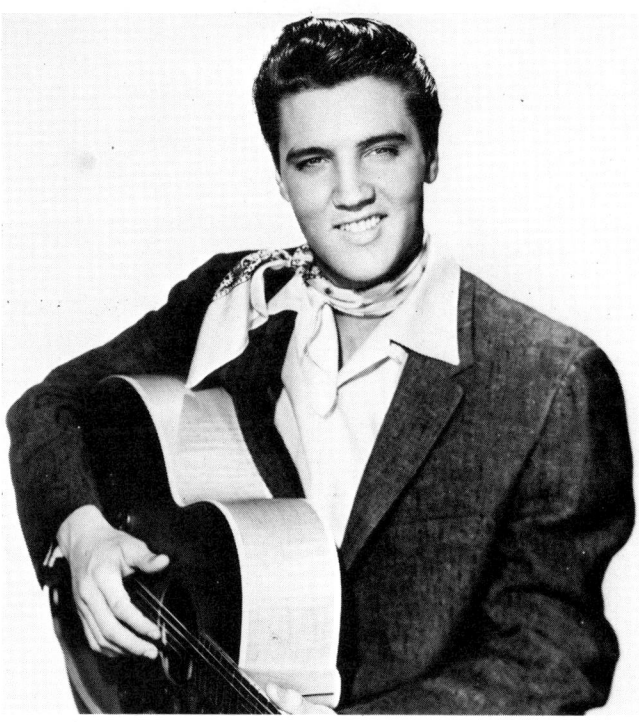

heavily shadowed, with a guitar in his hands. He is reconciled with his father, who is watching the performance, and he also has his true love in the audience, namely Dolores Hart. He lifts up his eyes, which are sparkling with tears, and he sings to his father, to his true love, to his audience, the very pertinent "As Long As I Have You". A most tearful finale.

An overdose of sentiment and some lurid melodramatics overpower *King Creole* in the end – but otherwise it does stand up. It precedes *West Side Story* as a "realistic" musical and is less embarrassing. Elvis gives a performance of finely graded animal naturalism – a consummate acting-singer acting well – and he does, beyond doubt, transcend the antiquated morality of the film's romantic main theme. And the film, besides being the best of his career, is a disturbing glimpse into the future, a drastic change of direction. It is obvious from viewing it that the rock is being dispensed with to build him up as a romantic ballad singer; thus all the rock songs are crammed into the excellent first half and the second half presents a new Elvis: the Family Favourite. For this reason, as distinct from the excellence of the whole production, it is the most crucial film of his career.

The changes in Elvis begin on television and are finally made manifest in Hollywood. He's been sweetened and groomed and convinced that he's an actor, and now he will leave rock behind. He will go into the army and do his two years and prove that he's as good as the rest of them. This period in his life (which costs the tax man a packet) is used as a platform for new things. So patriotic is the country, so obsessed with his image, that they see in his service, in his willingness to do it, a man whom any parents could respect.

His hair is cut short, he suddenly looks like your own son, and it is obvious that beneath all the glitter he is just like the rest of us. Then his mother dies, he weeps brokenly and publicly, and after this there is no one against him: he is pure as the driven snow. And so all this is used, with a fine sense of timing, to set him up as a good decent boy, as a man all the family can see.

Elvis Presley becomes a Matinée Idol.

King Creole marked the end of the "rebel" Elvis. *Opposite: With Dolores Hart and, above her, Carolyn Jones. Above: A new "mature" Elvis in a publicity still from the film.*

from loss of blood, and is rescued by the repentant Carolyn. She drives him to her hideaway, a shack by the sea, and together they share an idyllic few days. Then Walter comes along with a pistol in his hand, shoots at Elvis and hits Carolyn instead. It is now Elvis's turn, but a dumb kid he once befriended drags Walter into the sea where, quite miraculously, he shoots himself. Carolyn gives a sweet dying speech.

The last touching scene has Elvis back in the King Creole,

I can't see my reflection in the water
I can't speak the sounds that show no pain
I can't hear the echo of my footsteps
I can't remember the sound of my own name
– Tomorrow is a Long Time, *Bob Dylan*

Elvis comes out of the army in 1960 and goes straight into middle-road show biz. The first thing he does is tape a show with Frank Sinatra at the Fontainebleau Hotel in Miami. He is deep in the mortuary of the purple-haired ladies and we're never to know if he likes it. His long locks have been shorn, he is made to wear a tuxedo, and he's told not to move while he sings: he is truly obedient. He sings his current hit – ''Stuck on You'' and ''Fame and Fortune'' – but considering the tuxedo and the command not to move they really aren't given that much elbow room. He then sings Sinatra's ''Witchcraft'', they both duet on ''Love Me Tender'', and the whole thing is really quite dreary - besides being ominous.

The first post-army LP is called *Elvis is Back* (1960) and it comes in a nice fold-out booklet. The booklet is decorated with pictures of Elvis in the army, but luckily the contents rise above these. Obviously carefully angled to cover most of his styles, the album utilises the songs of Jerry Leiber and Mike Stoller, Stan Kesler and Otis Blackwell, blues writers Jesse Stone and Lowell Fulson, and it's beautifully produced. It also includes, by way of nods to the mainstream, fresh versions of Peggy Lee's ''Fever'' and Johnny Ray's ''Such a Night''. To challenge Peggy Lee is a challenge indeed, but the Presley version is smooth and very sexy, just as good as the original. As for the Johnny Ray number, which Ray handled dead-pan, Elvis bucks up the pace, salts the sex with some humour, and turns it into something immaculate. He also sings a few ballads, some foot-tapping rock and three genuinely exciting blues chanters. The voice is now deeper, much smoother and more assured, but it still manages to work wonders with insinuation

89

G. I. Blues *(1960). Above and opposite page: With Juliet Prowse. Right: with Harris Strickland Jnr. and cousin Paul Morgan in the Fontainebleau Hotel, Miami, before the Sinatra TV Special.*

and wit on such items as ''Stuck on You'' and ''Such a Night''. It is a promising return.

His first post-army single is received by many people as a definite statement of intent. He sings ''I'm stuck on you'' to a lovely rocking beat and it thunders up the charts as expected. But the following single is a remarkable turnaround – an updated version of the operatic ''O Sole Mio'' – and since this one, a non-rocker, is played on numerous mainstream stations,

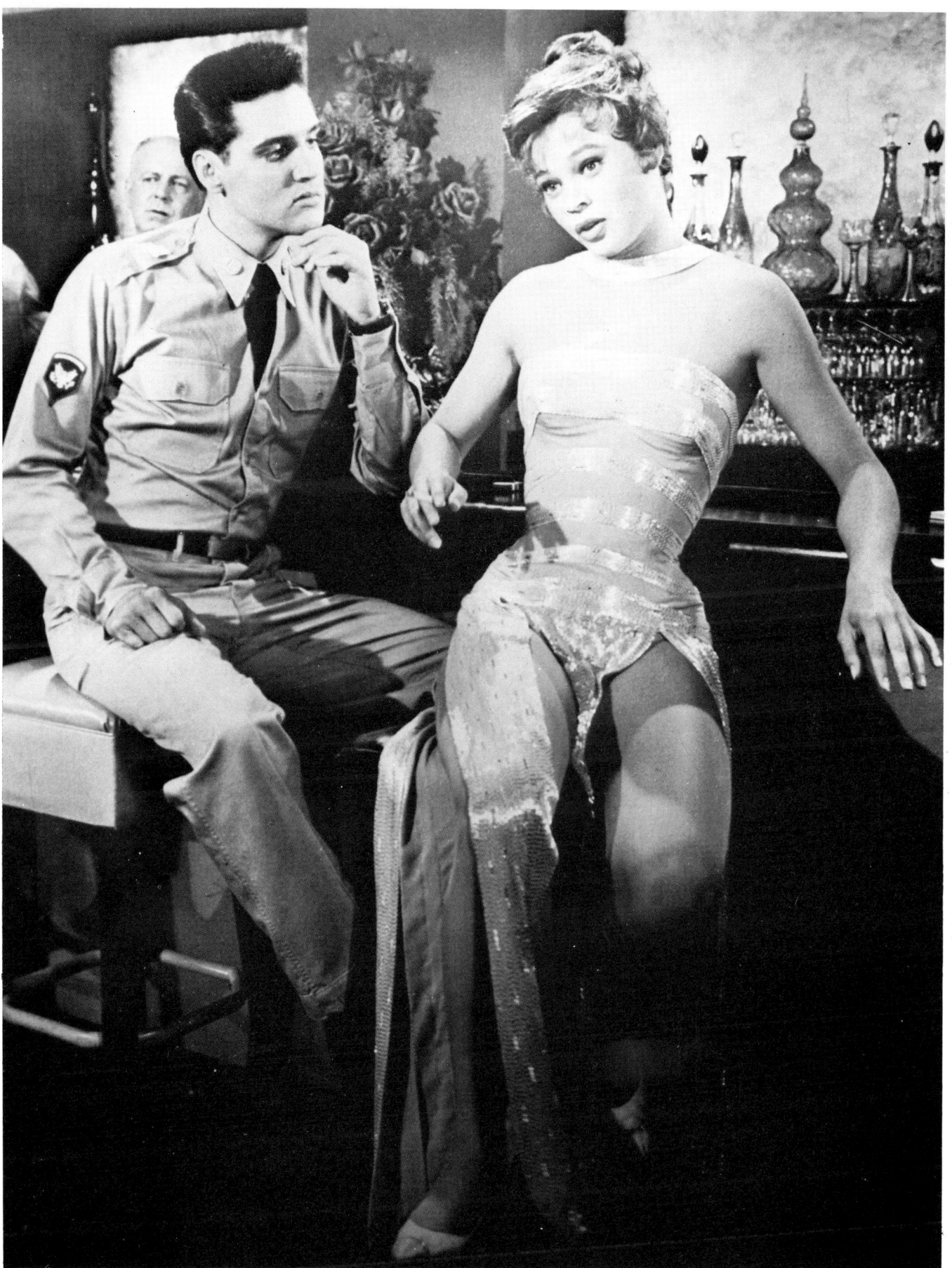

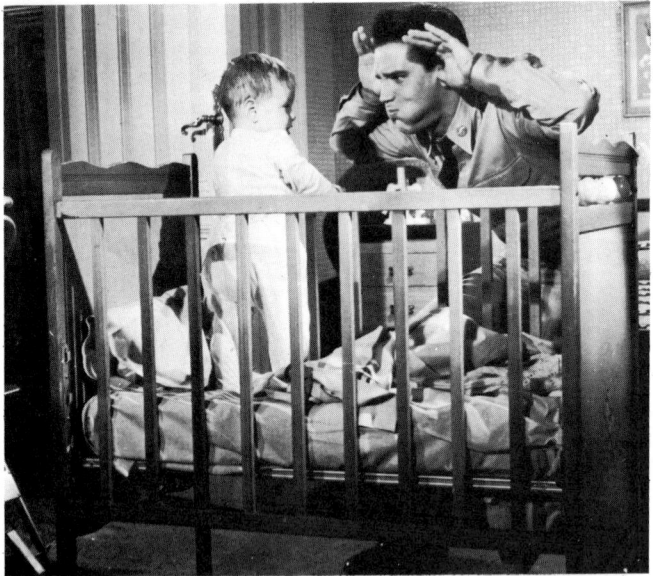

it becomes one of the biggest grossers ever. His next single, therefore, is "Are You Lonesome Tonight", an old Al Jolson weepy that was also once recorded by the Ink Spots. Elvis and the Jordanaires simply imitate the Ink Spots, but add the novelty of a soulful spoken bridge: sales-wise, it's a monster. And if there are still any doubts as to what direction Elvis is headed, his first post-army movie will resolve them.

G. I. Blues (1960) is first and foremost an exploitation movie that cashes in on Elvis's two years of service. It marks the true debut of the "family" movies and it isn't embarrassed to show

it. Elvis sings in beer gardens, in cable cars and trains, sings to children and puppets and the army, *looks after babies*. He also wears a soldier's uniform, drives a tank and tours the Rhineland, and falls in love with a sexy German dancer. This girl is Juliet Prowse and she walks away with the movie by performing an erotically charged dance that makes Elvis look tame. As for Elvis's rock numbers, they are few and far between and none of them is anything special. "Shoppin' Around" is a smooth and infectuous toe-tapper, but Elvis doesn't move much beyond some shoulder shrugging. "Frankfurt Special" is better, a sharp, snappy chanter, but it's performed while he's sitting in a train, surrounded by buddies. As for the title tune, it's as far removed from the blues as the earth is from Alpha Centauri; it is, in point of fact, one of the first really bad songs that have obviously come off the conveyor belt. Elvis's mode of presentation is to sing in deep voice while his buddies, all

G. I. Blues *was Elvis's first post-army movie and these scenes*
more or less speak for themselves. The sideburns cropped off,
the face well-fed and clean, he sings to puppets and children
and ladies, then finally bolsters the morale of the army. The
musicians are actually actors, the plot is pure Doris Day, and
the whole dismal affair makes a fortune. Elvis, perhaps
sensing the trap he was falling into, then attempted to make
two serious movies. The first one was Flaming Star *(1961), a*
Don Siegal western in which Elvis portraying a bitter half-
breed Indian (right) gave his finest screen performance. The
following pages demonstrate how well he suited the role – but
he only sang two songs (one over the credits) and thus the
film didn't do as well as the previous ones. Still, it remains
one of his best.

musicians, chant ''Hup-two-three-four'' as if they're practising
their drill in a slime pit. His leg movements, God help us, are a
simulated army march and his guitar is not synchronised to the
soundtrack. The last song, ''Didja Ever'', utilises the Stars and
Stripes, and it has to be heard to be believed. The movie makes
a fortune and its most popular moment is when Elvis sings
''Wooden Heart'' to the puppets. This becomes a hit single.

This film is the model around which the later films will be
based: some comedy, some love interest, some children, some
nice scenery and a handful of ''situation'' songs. Later, in
desperation, they'll add motor cars and boats, motor bikes and
aeroplanes, some animals and a lot of plastic girls, most of them
virginal. As for Elvis himself, he'll be gradually castrated into
an everlasting pubescent boy. And as movie follows movie,
each one worse than the last, he will actually start resembling a
eunuch: a plump, jittery figure. Meanwhile, his fans will wear
suits and buy houses, clip their hair and move back into steady
jobs while a whole new generation of young people will get
hip on revolution. Yes, the youth culture that he started will
flourish and grow while Elvis starts to rub noses with droopy

dogs, hold hands with virgin girls. At the moment, however, he hasn't quite sunk that far, and is about to take a last daring gamble.

It is possible that at this point he actually sees what is happening and attempts to break out of the trap. He has always been serious in his desire to be an actor – was in fact more excited by the good reviews of *King Creole* than by anything else in his career – and he might therefore have viewed *G. I. Blues* as mere commerce, as a means of reinstating his drawing

power. Packed with songs, full of colour, with just a little bit of everything, it will reach a wider audience than he ever had before and will consequently give him some leverage. It is not certain, but it is possible. If he makes this one sure thing, then the gates will be opened and he can tackle anything he desires: even try serious acting. So he makes his family movie called *G. I. Blues,* and it's a monster and he gets what he wants. He tries a couple of serious ones.

In both *Flaming Star* and *Wild in the Country* his potential is grasped. The former is based on a screenplay by Clair Huffaker and Nunnally Johnson, directed by the excellent Don Siegel, and includes in its cast Dolores Del Rio, Richard Jaeckel and John McIntyre: a notable crew. The latter is, if anything, even more extravagant in its credentials, being based on a superb novel by J. R. Salamanca, written up for the screen by Clifford Odets, produced by Jerry Wald, directed by Philip Dunne, featuring Tuesday Weld, Hope Lange, Millie Perkins and John Ireland, and with music by Kenyon Hopkins. It can be said of

both movies, though neither is perfect, that they seriously present Elvis with a challenge and help him to meet it.

In *Flaming Star* (1960) Elvis is the half-breed son of a full-blooded Indian and a white man. Brought up in the white community, he is agonizingly conscious of the problems that his mixed blood presents; when the Indians go to war against the whites, he is forced to choose between conflicting loyalties. In setting up this situation, the film zeros in neatly on Presley's own personal attributes: he is moody, violent and possessed of an animal grace; he is volatile yet strangely dignified. And Elvis's performance, if not up to Brando standards (the part was in fact originally conceived for Brando) still manages to convey, with a fine sense of balance, the pained dilemma of the man who doesn't belong anywhere – society's outsider.

In *Wild in the Country* (1961) he's again an outsider, but this time the conception, from the production roots up, is somewhat less than convincing. In all fairness to Elvis, the problem isn't in his performance, but in a surprisingly banal screenplay by Clifford Odets. Cast very much in the "Peyton Place" mould, it has Elvis as a young man with a personal history of violence and a latent talent (if not genius) for writing. Included in this steamy saga of small-town gallivantings is a love-stricken psychiatrist, a drunken uncle, a sex-crazy cousin, a sadistic father, a virginal lover, one near murder, one near suicide and numerous other entertaining sub-plots – quite a peppery stew. It does, however, present Elvis with the role that suits him well: once more he is moody and rebellious and romantic, a beautiful young dreamer whose pent-up violence is but a sign of his frustrated creativity. It's a hoary old theme, but it's expertly produced, and though Elvis is surrounded by a team of professionals, it is he and he alone who carries the film.

Flaming Star *(above) was followed by* Wild in the Country *(1961). A sombre movie with many serious flaws, it was enlivened by the presence of Elvis and sexy blond Tuesday Weld.*

The critics praise him again, but though the films make money they are, compared to his more musical efforts, relative duds.

Now the mystery resides in who makes his decisions: is Elvis himself so cut up by the failure that he simply can't face the loss of audience? Or is it (and on this his fans will definitely lay the blame) his management that now sings the new tune?

The most interesting myth is that his manager is all powerful, having a hold over Elvis that no one comprehends, but a hold that somehow can't be broken. Certainly, in later years, Elvis will appear so passive as to be positively devoid of all volition – a mere functioning machine. If he does what Parker says, even if Parker was to wreck his career, well, so be it, he will not stoop to argue, he will row the boat. It is, in its intricate and intriguing possibilities, one of the more enduring riddles in pop – no one yet knows the answer. But whatever the reasons, Elvis is now about to embark upon a voyage into artistic failure, into the darkest backwaters of the most sublime mediocrity. Yes, if Elvis stops singing the cash register stops ringing; so from now on he will sing and be most sympathetic – and there ain't another thing to discuss.

Hollywood spreads its tarnished wings.

Already he has considerably cut back on his non-film recordings. He releases *His Hand in Mine* (1960), an LP of religious songs, and most of it is really outstanding. But as far as singles go, he offers only "Wooden Heart", and "Surrender", another rehashed Italian song, albeit sung superbly. The next single will be the title tune of *Wild in the Country,* a modest little ballad heading nowhere. It is backed by a great version of "I Feel So Bad", a rocking Chuck Willis blues number. But this side is buried, not approved of by his new fans, and might well be a fresh nail in his coffin. He will shortly release a rocker, the excellent "Little Sister", backed by the more

Opposite page and first left: Elvis as a serious actor takes his final bow in Wild in the Country. *Below left: A rare shot of Elvis in white dinner jacket during a personal appearance at a benefit show in the Ellis Auditorium in Memphis, 25 February, 1961. On 26 March, 1961, he flew to Hawaii for another public appearance in Pearl Harbor's huge Bloch Arena. He did a very long show, moved around quite a bit, and finished with sweat on his brow. As the photos below demonstrate, he pulled in some old friends to accompany him. Behind him in the Memphis shot is J. D. Fontana on drums. In the Hawaiian shots the saxaphonist is Boots Randolph and the guitarist is the legendary Scotty Moore. The Hawaiian show was his farewell performance. He remained there to make* Blue Hawaii *(overleaf), then went home for a string of awful movies, not to be seen "live" again for another 8 years.*

popular "His Latest Flame". Neither record will do as well as the smooth, rhythmic ballads, and doubtless this will reinforce decisions.

In February, 1961, he makes a personal appearance at two benefit shows in the Ellis Auditorium in Memphis. It is the first time he has done so since his discharge from the army, but it isn't the good sign that it seems. He wears a white dinner jacket, black trousers and tie, and this time he doesn't get himself moist: he is cool and sophisticated.

A couple of weeks later he flies to Hawaii for another public appearance, this time in Pearl Harbor's Bloch Arena. He can't start for five minutes because of the hysteria, but when he gets going he is very smooth indeed. He wears a gold lamé jacket, an open-neck shirt, and has a garland of flowers around his neck. He sings "Heartbreak Hotel", "Such a Night", "Don't be Cruel", "Treat me Nice", "All Shook

Up", "It's Now or Never", "That's All Right", "Are You Lonesome Tonight", "Hound Dog" and quite a few others. He sings loud and clear, the back-up band is excellent, but it's all very much tongue in cheek: he is mocking himself. And who knows at this time – who would want to believe it – that it's to be his last public appearance for a long, bleak, eight years?

Who knows, indeed? From this point onward the course of his career will defy all effective analysis. Certainly, for someone so inherently outrageous, he will show a stunning lack of resistance, a mystifying compliance.

Some will say that his love for his mother was so strong that her death drained the interest right out of him: he did, after all, only do it for her, to rescue her from the poverty of her life, give her some nice things. There is also the common knowledge that when fame overtook him, his mother couldn't handle it, felt dislocated from her background and frequently displayed real signs of stress, including diet pills and alcohol. If this be true, then it is very possible that he holds himself

Above: Blue Hawaii *(1961) marked the beginning of the second-rate films. Opposite: Surprisingly,* Follow That Dream *(1962) was one of the funniest of the year. Colonel Parker, being held up at gun-point, was* not *in this film.*

responsible for her death; and, with her passing, suffers not only her loss but the ever-gnawing pain of his secret guilt. It is a reasonable, if not too pleasant theory.

Others, less romantic, will say that his management is antiquated to the point of senility. As we know his management is, for the most part, a bizarre one-man band dominated by the flamboyant Colonel Parker. An ex-circus barker, a legendary wheeler-dealer, he was great in the days when pure corn was a commodity, but is now out of touch with reality. He still thinks that show business is the domain of the family audience, and that sweetness and light, with some ludicrous gimmicks, will continue to bring the money in. And it is this Svengali, both cunning and benign, this extraordinary show-man-salesman of the decaying American South who is selling

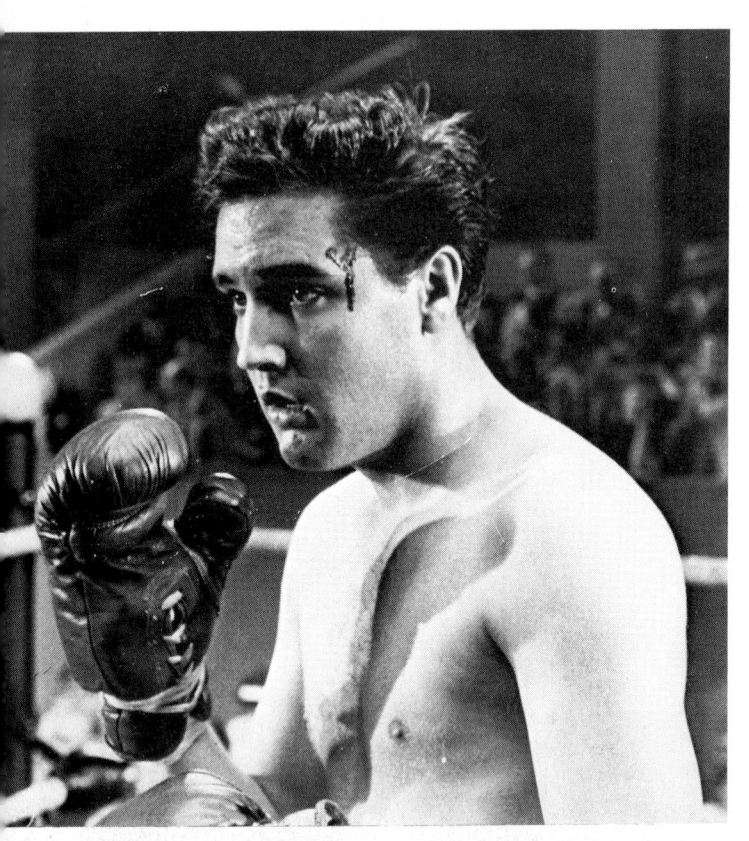

Opposite page: The seeds of confusion obviously began to sprout in Kid Galahad *(1962). Another attempt at blending a "serious" story with some songs, it failed miserably from the first reel to the last. Nor did it fare too well at the box office. By way of atonement, Elvis's next film was again set in his profitable blue Hawaii. It was called* Girls! Girls! Girls! *(1962) and it was every bit as silly as its title. Still, it made a fortune at the box office and thus set the format of future films: cute children, gorgeous gals, exotic locales and lots of songs – all filmed in glorious colour for matinée viewing.* Girls! Girls! Girls! *(this page) had a little bit of everything, and it was a monster in the cinemas and on vinyl. Hereafter the films would become interchangeable – as the pictures on the following pages demonstrate.*

Elvis off, like his popcorn and balloons, on the safest lines imaginable.

Certainly it is true that Parker doesn't read film scripts, doesn't care for the contents, and will only discuss cash at the conference table: he is that sort of manager. But this still begs the question of why Elvis himself, at the height of his success, and certainly with enough drawing power to call his own shots, seems to hand it all over without a word. No matter how bad the movies, no matter how low his record sales, he lets it happen with no sign of resistance – he is passive, a living ghost.

For the moment, however, he is still in Hawaii, to soak in the sun and make the first of the real trash. It's called *Blue Hawaii* (1961), and it's utterly abysmal, but it's packed with sweet songs (pastiche Hawaiian ballads) and the scenery is quite gorgeous to city folk. Needless to say, it's a box-office monster – and not only that, but the soundtrack album becomes the biggest-selling item he's ever had. So this all-singing, girl-chasing, virginal Elvis, in his swimming trucks and thongs, with his surf boards and sports cars, has just proven that the mean lad of *Flaming Star* and *Wild in the Country* is not what the good folks out there want. No, they want a nice travelogue, filled with songs and sexy gals, and they don't want anything that might threaten them. In short, they want escapism.

As if to prove this point, our good clean boy's next movie is a modest little comedy set in Florida. Called *Follow That Dream* (1962), it has Elvis as the bumbling son of a family of entertaining rural nutters. It is really very funny, with Elvis near perfect, showing a natural flair for comedy and timing. But it isn't glamorous enough, there are only a few songs, and it doesn't do much at the box office. He follows it up with a pedestrian remake of *Kid Galahad* (1962), and again, though

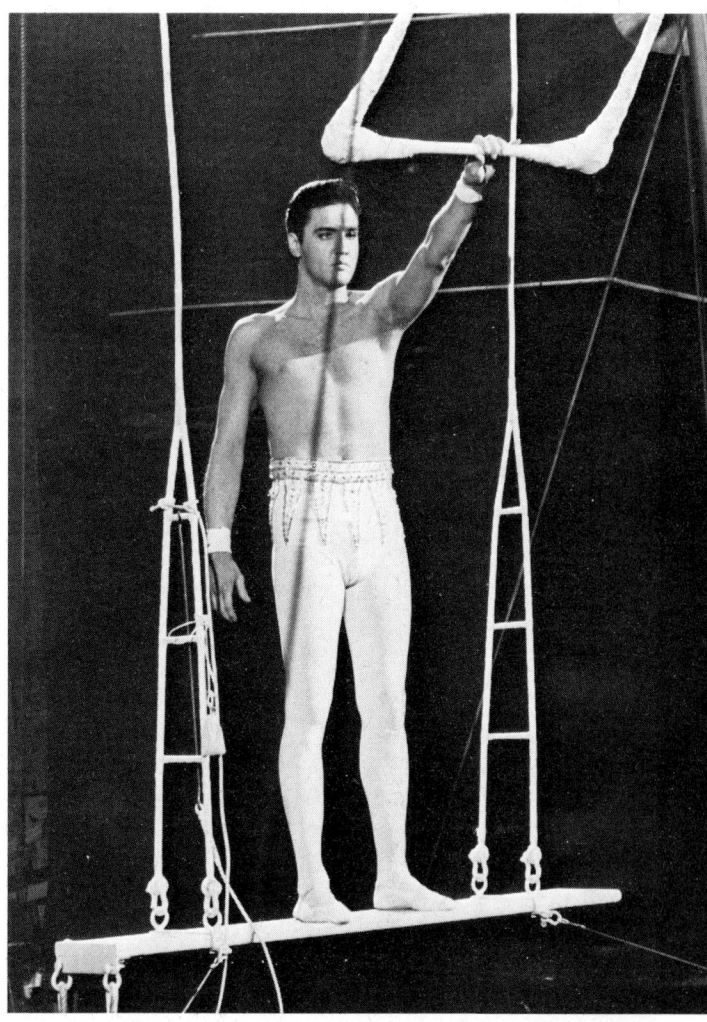

Above and top of opposite page: Kissin' Cousins *(1964).*
Right and bottom of opposite page (with Ursula Andress):
Fun in Acapulco *(1963). Below and bottom right:* It
Happened at the World's Fair *(1963).*

he is good, there are very few songs and the background is
hardly a paradise. It gets a reasonable audience, but it's no
Blue Hawaii – and that's enough news for everyone concerned.
He is rushed straight back to Hawaii, quickly makes *Girls!
Girls! Girls!* (1962) and it's a monster in the cinemas and on
vinyl.

A point has been proved.

For the next seven years, while the real world explodes,
he'll make an average of three films a year, most of them
ludicrous. In few of them will he play a professional singer:
he'll just be a guy who sings for his kicks and some extra
bread. In all of them he'll be engaged in the pursuit of pretty
girls, none of whom will he take to bed. In most there'll be a
fist fight, some children, some animals, and some glittering
machinery: it's the affluent age. And in none will he play
a nasty role – he will always be a bland and straightforward
boy.

The films will degenerate from a reasonable level of com-
petence to the most appalling display of indifference. Written,
produced and directed by hacks, they will stink from the

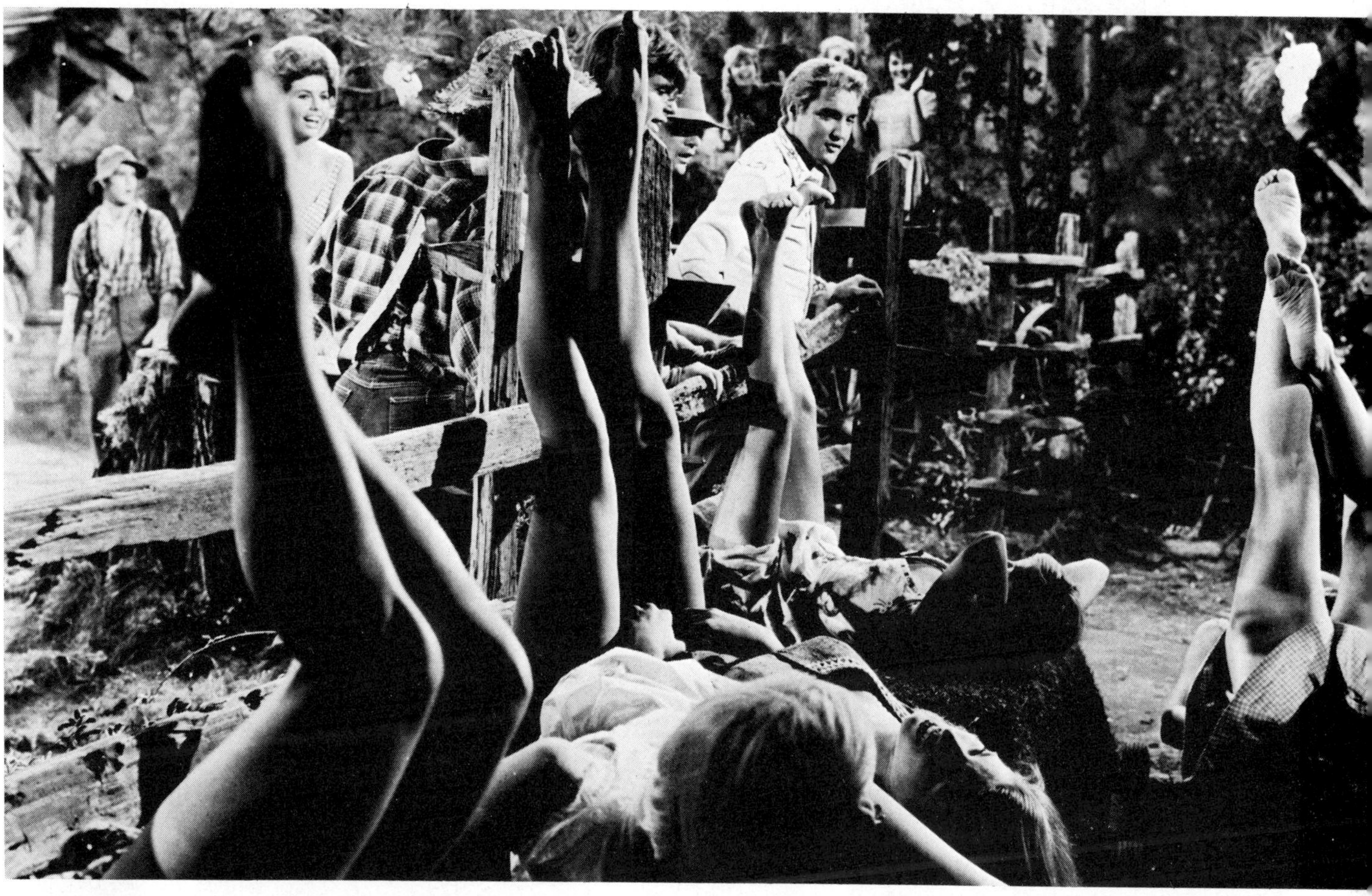

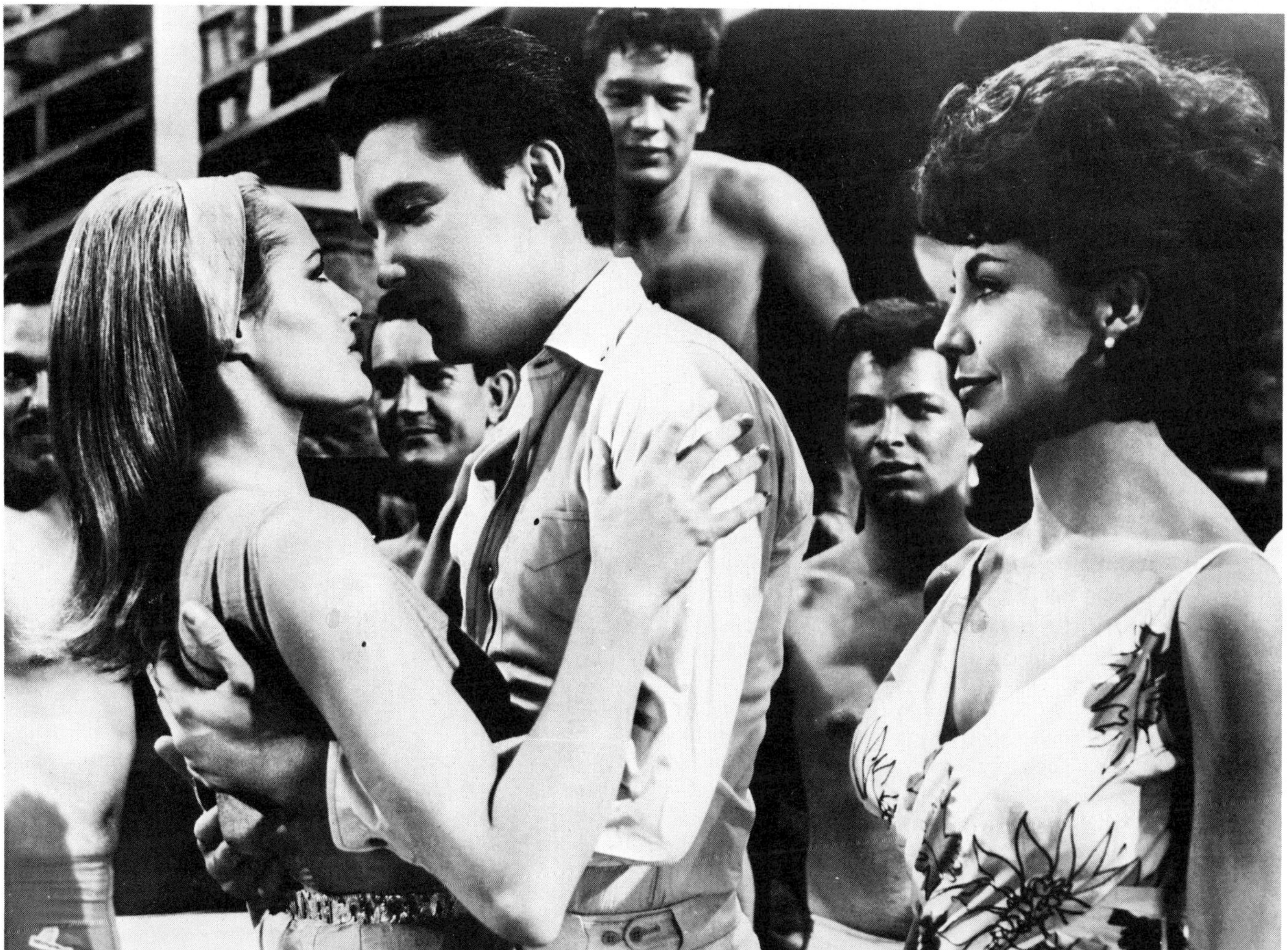

credits to the last mindless reel with the stench of their own appalling taste. Some very talented players will wander through these wastelands, looking desperate or dazed or simply cynical. And the star himself, as if not quite believing it, will finally start parroting his lines like a man in a waking dream – and in the end actually develops a twitch that resembles nothing short of nervous spasms. He will grow fat and lazy, monumentally bored, and as the films pile up like more stones on his grave, he'll recede farther back into the shelter of Graceland, back into his mysterious and shadowed thoughts, back to his memories.

The last remotely decent film is *Viva Las Vegas!* (1964), and it is even more successful than *Blue Hawaii*. They take their

A lightweight affair, but still his best musical in years, was Viva Las Vegas! *(1964). The Las Vegas locale enabled them to put in some rock songs – and Ann-Margret, whose image is similar to Elvis's, was a bonus.*

time shooting it, the songs are well presented, and Elvis and his co-star, the sexy Ann-Margret, form the most attractive twosome in years. It is even quite possible that the challenging Miss Margret briefly lifts him from the doldrums he's been in; most certainly when they double (as in the very good "C'mon Everybody" sequence) the fireworks explode loud and bright. Both performers are sinuous and sensual and assured, and between them they manage to lift a routine movie far above what it would otherwise be. But it also has the bonus of director George Sidney – and it's the last one that will be so blessed. From now on it is Deadsville.

Parker's only concern is that each film should make an album that can later be flogged off like toothpaste; for this reason, his only interest in the script is that it leave blanks for

songs. The songs are mostly ghastly, pure "situation" fodder, knocked together fast in some computerised back room and often manufactured around no more than the title – which itself is frequently murderous. What do you do when you're told to write a song called "There's No Room To Rhumba in a Sports Car"? Godammit, you do it. And bearing in mind that it's Elvis, and that the boy's got some tonsils, you try some pastiche rock, some mock country ballads, some calypso, some modernised oldies and some operatic rewrites – it's all grist to the mill.

The titles of these songs are, in themselves, a most illuminating summary of their contents: "Ito Eats", "Beach Shack", "Smorgasboard", "Wolf Call", "Adam and Evil", "Do The

The best part of Viva Las Vegas! *was the "C'mon Everybody" routine. Above: A respectable Elvis in Graceland.*

109

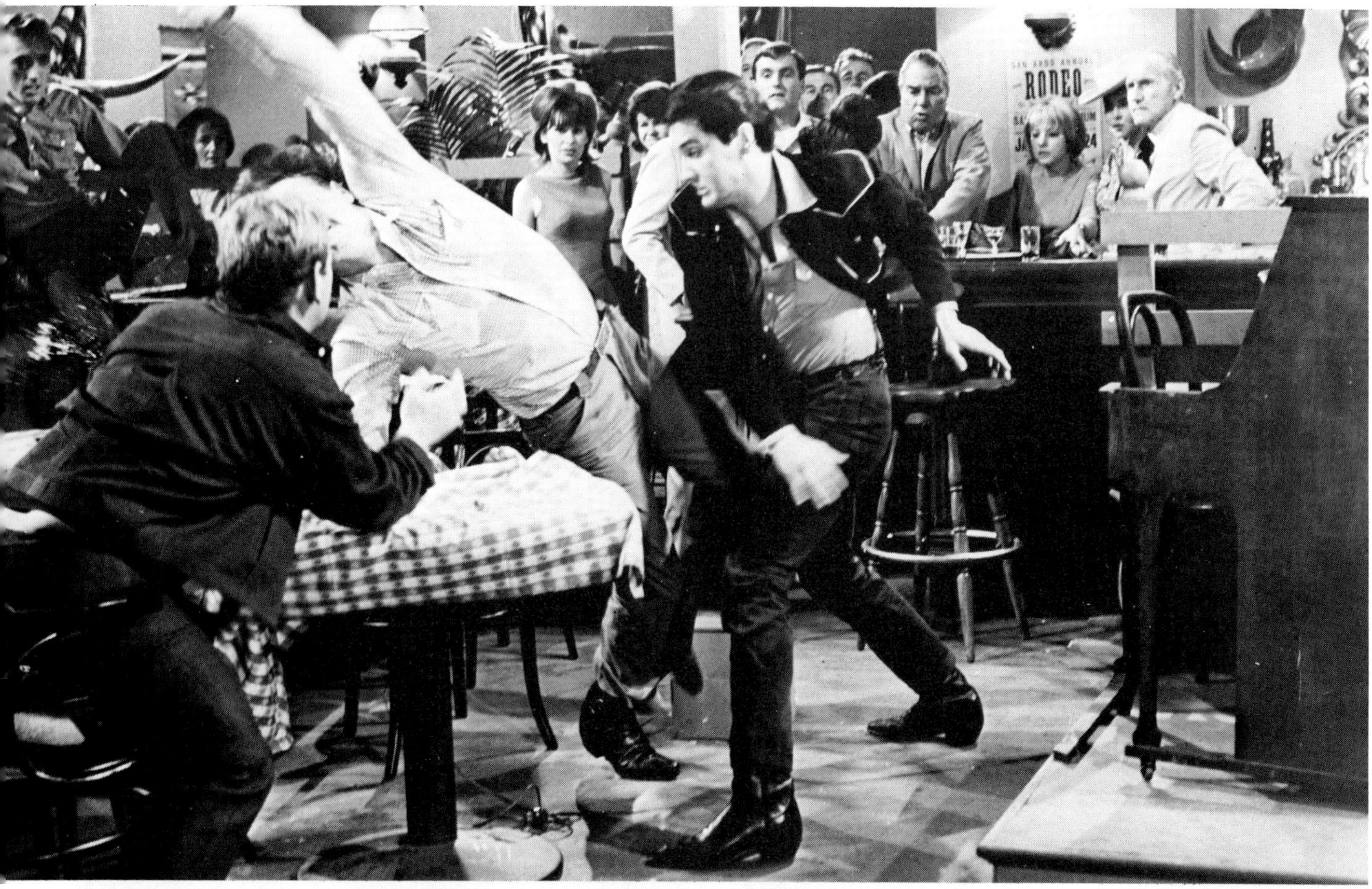
RODEO

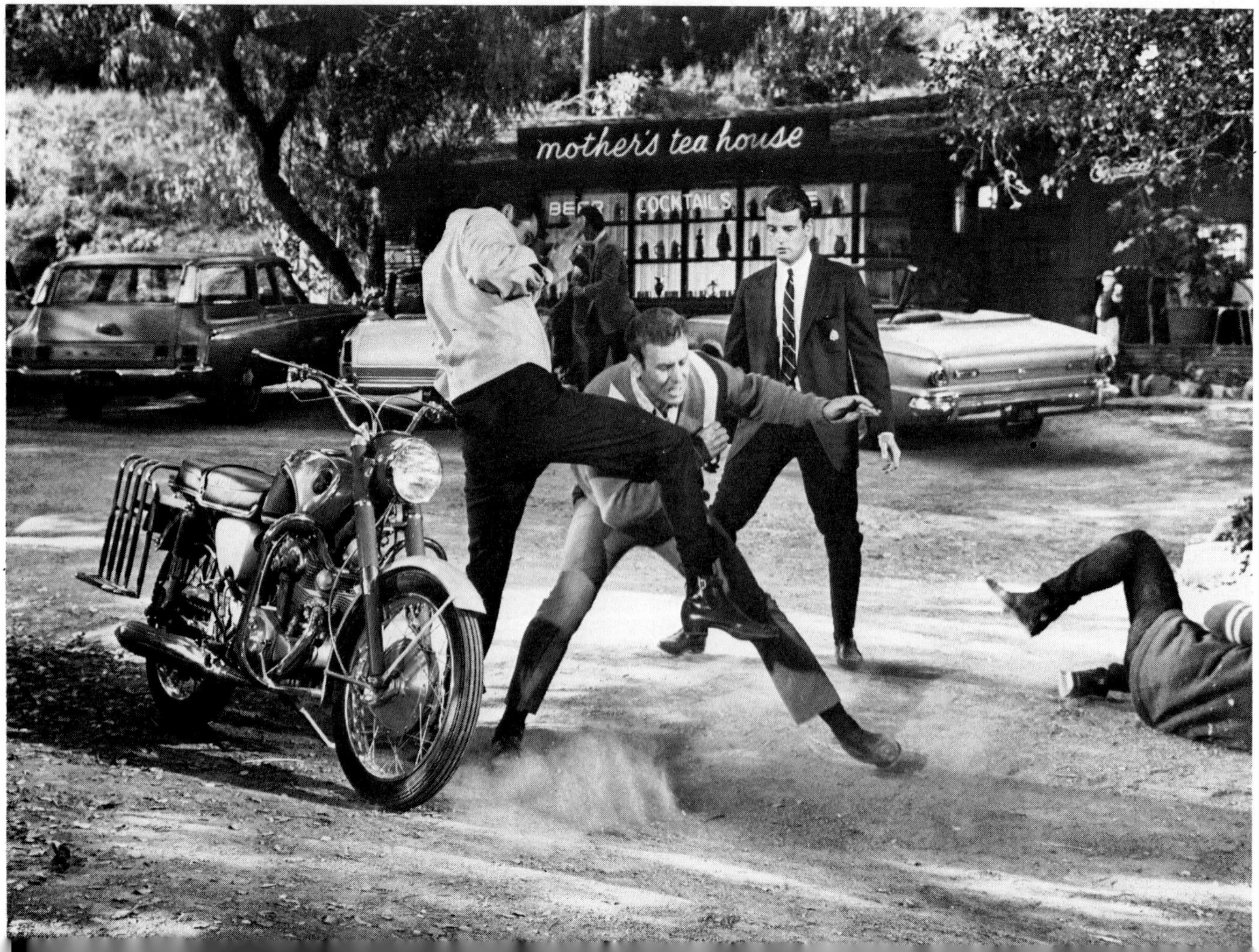
mother's tea house
COCKTAILS

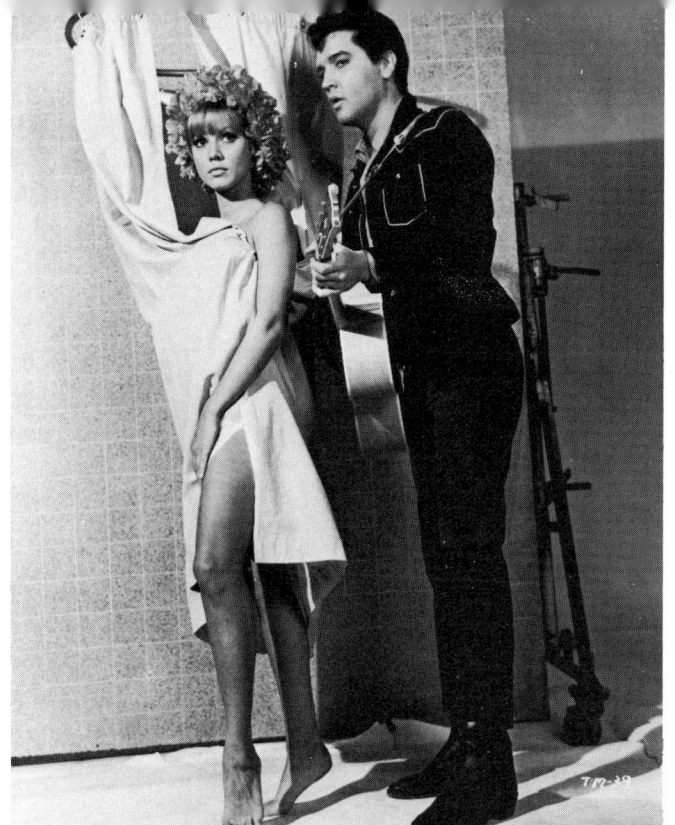

Opposite page, top, he punches someone in Tickle Me *(1965). Bottom, he kicks someone in* Roustabout *(1964). Above, he wrecks a bar in* Girl Happy *(1965). Top left, Jocelyn Lane in* Tickle Me; *top right, Mary Ann Mobley in* Girl Happy.

Clam'', ''Shake That Tambourine'', ''Go East Young Man'', ''Yoga Is as Yoga Does'', ''Petunia, The Gardener's Daughter'', ''Fort Lauderdale Chamber of Commerce'' and, most delicious, a song in itself, the remarkable ''Long Legged Girl With The Short Dress On'' – a real mind-blower. As for the revamped golden oldies, he tries ''Santa Lucia'', ''Old MacDonald's

Farm'', ''Down by the Riverside'', ''When the Saints Go Marching In'', ''The Eyes of Texas'' and ''The Yellow Rose of Texas'' amongst numerous others.

When they fall short on these gems they pad out the albums with a novelty now known as ''bonus'' songs. Since these so-called ''bonus'' songs are pure studio recordings, they are by

Elvis in striped coat playing Johnny in Frankie and Johnny *(1966). The Oriental costume is for* Harum Scarum *(1965) and he's surrounded by Mary Ann Mobley (left of picture) and Fran Jeffries. Marianna Hill flashes her legs in* Paradise, Hawaiian Style *(1966); Suzanna Leigh (above) in same flick.*

far the best things he is doing. Perhaps out of a desperation born from singing movie trash, he now concentrates during his rare serious sessions on shaping himself into a crystalline ballad singer – and he succeeds. A phase of his career that is largely ignored, it nevertheless shows that he has not lost his love of singing; that given the right material and some genuine interest he can still manage to convey, with masterly control, a very real sense of human loss and nobility. Starting with his beautiful rendition of "Falling in Love with You", he will continue in this vein with such lovely ballads as "Forget Me Never", "I Need Somebody to Lean On", "Please Don't Stop Loving Me", "I'll Remember You" and his exquisite interpretation of "Love Letters". Unfortunately, so bad is the general quality of the soundtracks that his work during this period, admittedly quite scarce, will be buried on the backs

As the films get worse, so do their titles. Above and opposite: Scenes from Easy Come, Easy Go *(1967) in which Elvis played an underwater demolition man. Top of opposite page is a typical fight from* Double Trouble *(1967).*

of albums that are no longer selling.

In the whole long eight years there will only be three albums of original, non-film material. The first one, *Pot Luck* (1962), is a rather strained attempt to cover most of his more popular singing styles – but his heart isn't in it. ''Kiss Me Quick'' is a dismal copy of his smash, ''It's Now or Never''; ''Just For Old Time Sake'' is a steal from ''Old Shep''; ''Easy

Question'' is a bid for the Dean Martin Trophy – and so it goes on for twelve tracks. The next album, three years later, is called *Elvis For Everyone* (1965), which means that it's a bag of leftovers. It includes throw-outs from *Wild in the Country*, *Viva Las Vegas*, *Flaming Star* and *Follow That Dream*. It also includes an excellent bluesy rendition of ''Tomorrow Night'', originally recorded in 1956; a superb howling blues, ''When

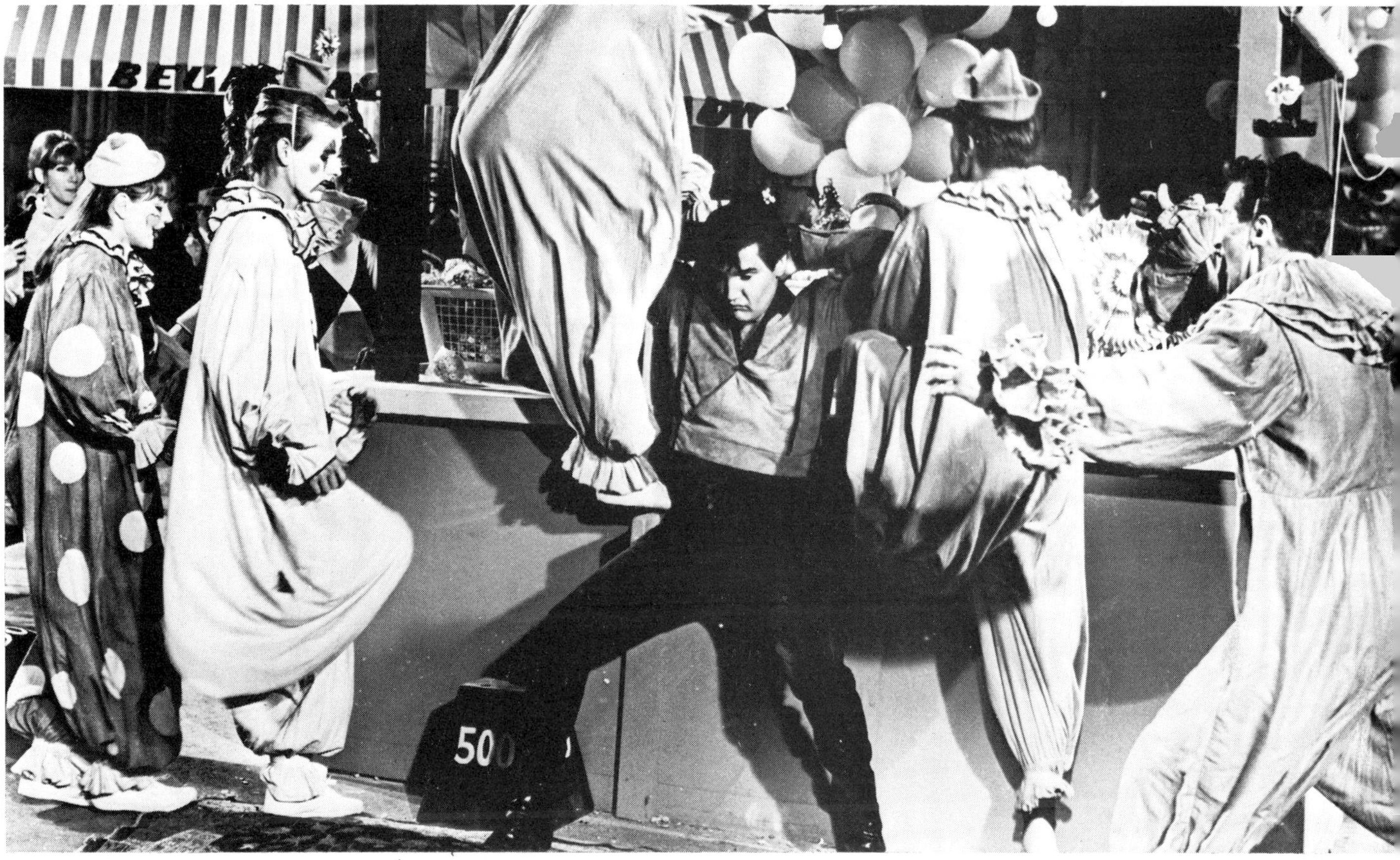
500

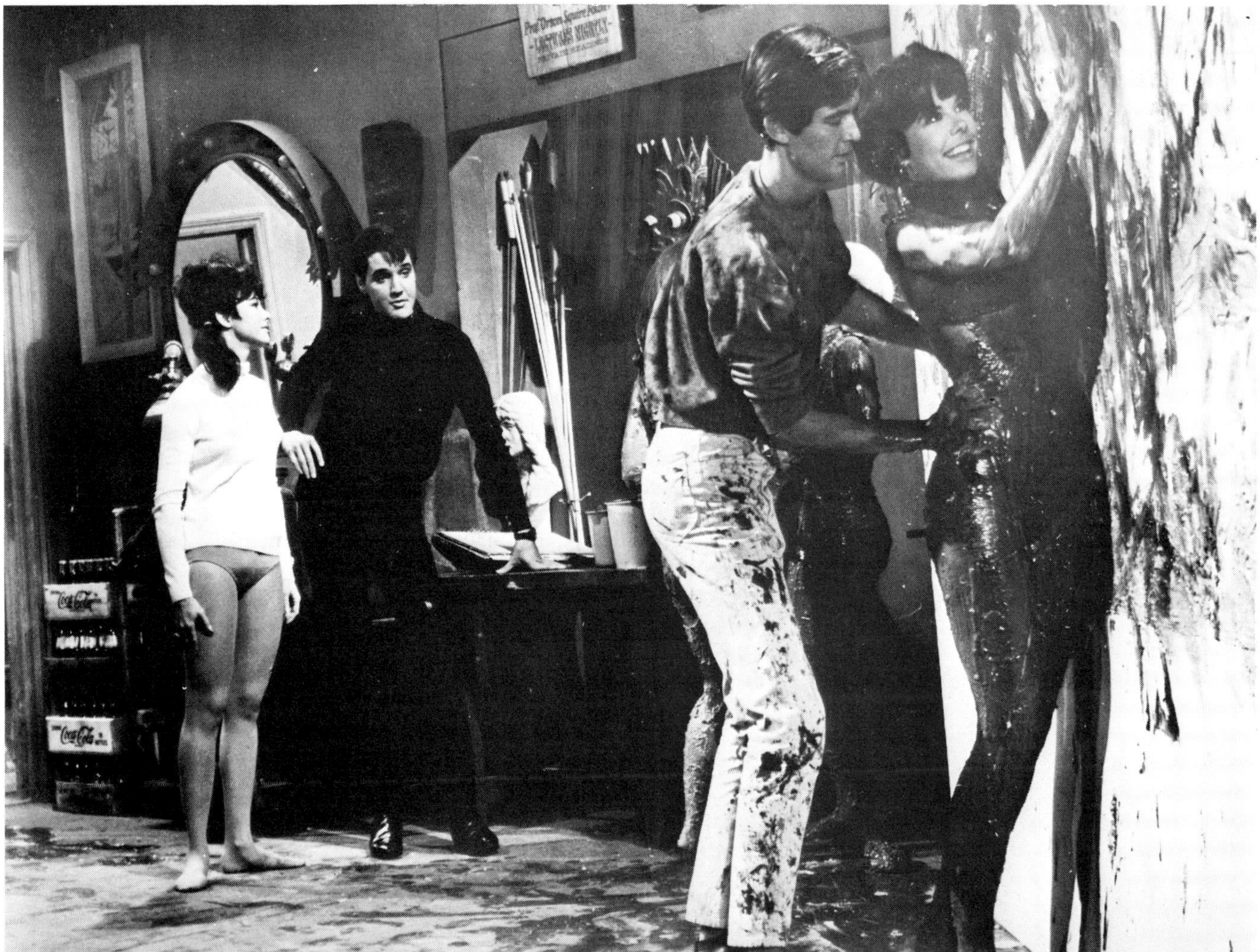
Coca-Cola
Coca-Cola

Below: Clambake *(1967) was a typical disaster, but no worse than* Spinout *(1966, see motorbike pic). Even worse was* Speedway *(1968, see disco photo).* Stay Away Joe *(1968, see the stetson) was a healthily bizarre curio.*

It Rains, It Really Pours'', originally recorded in 1957; ''Memphis Tennessee,'' originally recorded in 1963; and a good, but obviously antique version of Hank Williams's ''Your Cheating Heart''. The third album of this period, released a good two years later, is *How Great Thou Art* (1967). A religious album, it is reasonable but doesn't match previous efforts and it seems that even his own favourite music cannot stir much enthusiasm now.

The films roll. He hides in Graceland.

His records rarely see the hit parade; his films are sinking. Now the movies take a fortnight from beginning to completion and are starting to go out as supporting features. He hides out

in his mansion and does nothing; Colonel Parker makes no move. Meanwhile, the world changes, becomes restless and more political, and popular music, to be popular, must reflect this. The Beatles come along to revitalise a dead scene, and Bob Dylan writes songs that eschew false romance and lash out with uncommon defiance. A great admirer of Presley's, he has obviously been influenced by his vocal tricks, his "shock" tactics and his rebellion. But Dylan's songs are more articulate, he is studiously non-conformist, and he will not be enslaved by "show business". He is, indeed, the new prophet of pop culture, and he sings to young people who despise glamour and ambition, Tin Pan Alley and Hollywood, who

demonstrate in the streets and on the campuses for political change. And so the new music follows Dylan, and the Beatles and the Stones, while their hero, Elvis Presley, now well fed and slick, makes strange movies with titles such as *Girl Happy*, *Tickle Me*, *Harum Scarum* and *Paradise, Hawaiian Style*. It's not real. *It's a weird scene, man.*

By this time Elvis must be suffering an enormous lack of self-confidence. He has seen himself tumble from the highest peaks of fame to an anonymity as total as the dungeon: it is close to a nightmare. Hiding out in hotels in Graceland, he is surrounded by his "ol' boys", by the voices of his childhood, and they play silly games and watch out for his moods and

The films don't improve, but the Elvis image does. A side-burned, trimmed down and white-suited Elvis brutally slaps Sheree North in the ridiculously entitled The Trouble With Girls and How to Get Into It *(1969). Below: Another punch-up in* Live A Little, Love A Little *(1968). Opposite: A 'different' Elvis in the ill-fated* Charro *(1969).*

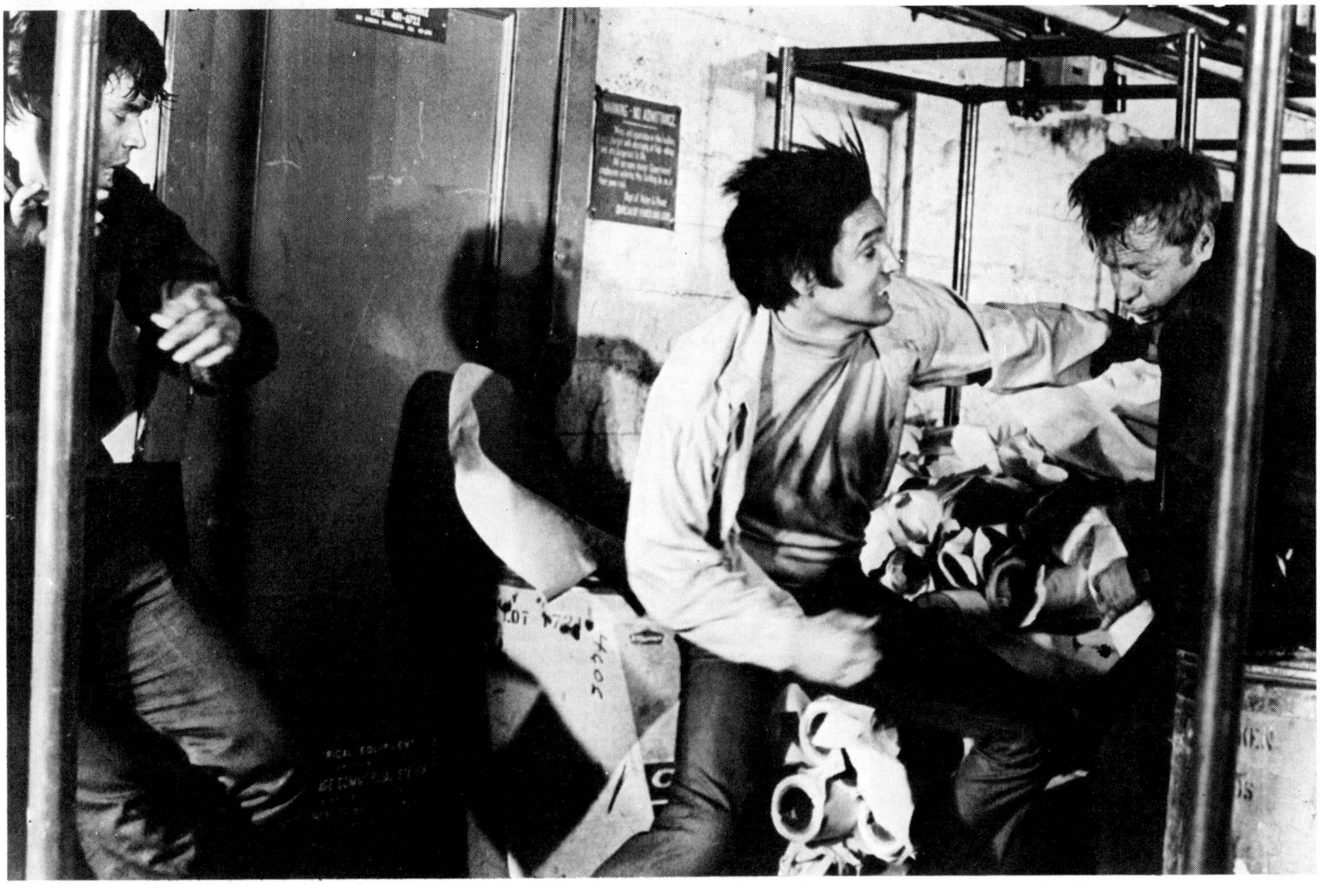

slip notes beneath his door when he locks himself in his room, often not seen for days. Sometimes, sitting in darkness, drumming his fingers as the clock on the wall ticks the hours by, the silence of the years slips around him and enfolds him in thin ice. Sometimes the boys get him out – play some ball, hire a funfair, shoot pistols at flash-bulbs in the pool – but this doesn't last long. He can be polite, or he can burn them with his eyes, ignore their very presence, and most often he retreats. And the fans come and go through the halls down below and start wondering if he ever existed, if he isn't mere fantasy.

What do you do when you have reached the very top before you've even taken a deep breath? Where can you go now? Elvis is rich beyond mere tabulation, yet he doesn't make much use of the money. True, he buys Cadillacs and supports a large crew; true, he lives in grand ostentation. But he never leaves America, has no lust to see the world, perhaps doesn't even know, in his solitude and paralysis, that the

outer world actually exists. Why does he not want to get out, to explore something fresh? – new musicians, new friends, new records, new countries. It never happens, and the mystery of his personality, once so vital and rich, thus spirals into more esoteric shores and leaves him stranded on barren rocks.

Some suspect he's just dumb, others think he's just jaded, yet others will say that his need to perform has been thwarted and is starting to throttle him. And so, as the years pass and he slips into history, he becomes, perversely and in his least productive period, a figure of almost mythical unreality, a folk hero, an idealised memory now frozen in the haze of a romantic past. "Remember *Elvis*?", they now say. "He *was* great." But the very fact of his disappearance, of his strange, oblique retirement, turns him into an American legend: another corrupted dream.

The films continue to come out at regular intervals, each one worse than the last. Elvis sings in settings made of

More scenes from Live A Little, Love A Little *(Elvis fighting and Elvis leering at the cardboard girl);* Charro *(Elvis with cigar and on horseback) and* The Trouble With Girls and How To Get Into It *(with the blonde, with the brunette).*

cardboard and plastic, he plugs a morality that went out ten years earlier, he prays at altars and romps in sports cars and splashes in water and chases girls, grinning like some huge dopey kid when they let him hold hands. When the songs are set up, he's surrounded by bikinis and guys who can't play their guitars. Though maybe he snaps his fingers, sways his hips just a little, he's embarrassed in a way he never had to be before. But he always wins his races, always marries his gal, and never opens his mouth without violins – a true, outmoded beach boy.

These films represent the very nadir of his career, but no

one ever works out why he does them. He is obviously under contract and that must count for something – but even starlets have been known to have tantrums. What few understand, and what many can't forgive, is that he never steps forward to complain. Stories emerge of his boredom and disgust, but no sign of revolt is forthcoming. He flies in for a fortnight, does his bit and gets out, back to study the gilt walls of Graceland and remember better days. It is life in a glass bowl; he has lived with the same people for near to thirty years and anything beyond them is alien, a world he can't handle. And now, it is said, he never looks you in the eye, mumbles his words, keeps his gaze on the floor, then drifts away like the ghost in the mansion, just looking for privacy.

Eight years, indeed, is a long time.

In the May of 1967 Elvis Presley is married. The girl is Priscilla Beaulieu, an old Memphis sweetheart. Nine months later, blessed day, they have a child and reality steps in.

Now he suddenly starts moving and no one quite knows the reason: whether becoming a father has given him back his drive, whether his manager has pulled off some extraordinary deal, or whether Elvis himself has finally vomited up the crap and is taking things into his own hands. No matter. He is changing.

The first change comes in September when he goes back to Nashville to cut some intelligent records. Included in this session are "Guitar Man", "Big Boss Man", "High Heel Sneakers" and "Just Call Me Lonesome" – all pertinent, all gutsy. The next noticeable change is in *Stay Away Joe* (1968), a zany little movie in which Elvis, once a nice boy, has a riotous time playing a contemporary Navajo Indian who smokes, drinks, jokes, sings, fights and does a lot of womanising – a considerable turnaround. Then, in another movie, *Live A Little, Love A Little* (1968), he actually shares a lady's bed and sports sideburns. Both movies sink fast, but the

Above and below: Change of Habit *(1969) gave Elvis his last acting role. Handsome, sideburned, he played an expensively dressed doctor slaving religiously in a Hollywood ghetto with a bunch of pretty nuns, one of whom he falls in love with. The film sank like a stone, but when it turned up on television, it was better than its synopsis would suggest – and Elvis's performance, if not particularly demanding, was fluid, relaxed and full of charm. He has not acted since. Top left opposite page: The new-look Elvis comes back with a bang in his 1968 NBC-TV Special. Top right: The sideburns creep downwards as can be seen in this shot where he talks to Colonel Parker on the set of his last film,* Change of Habit. *Bottom left: Elvis, on horseback, comes out of seclusion to meet fans in the grounds of Graceland. Finally (bottom right), a sideburned, trimmed-down Elvis is about to enter the seventies.*

point has been made, and in *Charro* (1969) the change is even more evident. A lousy Western film with some very phoney sets, it nevertheless has Elvis looking brutish and unshaven, and its one song is buried behind the credits. Elvis doesn't act well, but then neither does anyone else, and the direction, to put it mildly, is basic. In his next film *The Trouble with Girls*, (1969), in which he might be described as a "guest" star, he wears a white suit, a brimmed hat and huge sideburns; and suggests to a lady, with a nice lop-sided grin, that they continue their conversation in bed.

He looks just like he used to.

The Presley resurrection, at the end of 1968, is as swift as

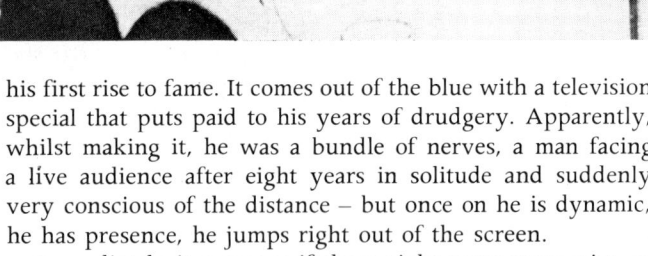

his first rise to fame. It comes out of the blue with a television special that puts paid to his years of drudgery. Apparently, whilst making it, he was a bundle of nerves, a man facing a live audience after eight years in solitude and suddenly very conscious of the distance – but once on he is dynamic, he has presence, he jumps right out of the screen.

Immediately it seems as if those eight years were mist, as if the Presley we knew had never really been away and had never let himself get out of touch. He looks extraordinarily different from his bland film persona, is remarkably handsome in his very tough way. And his voice which in Hollywood was "that curious baritone" is now raunchy and sensual and threatening: a miraculous revival.

Sometimes dressed in black leather, sometimes wearing a white suit, he moves his body with the lithe grace and finely tuned instincts of a performer in total command of what he is and what he can do. And in the selection of songs, in their mode of presentation, he wipes the floor with his rivals.

The world sits up and blinks, shakes its head in disbelief, then rushes out to snap up the soundtrack album. The closing song, "If I Can Dream", is pushed out as a single and becomes a million-seller in no time. Elvis then goes back to Memphis for the first time in fourteen years and sweats through his most productive session ever. Backed up by real musicians and some genuine songs, he sums up his career and then puts out an album, *From Elvis in Memphis* (1969), that is one of the best he has ever done. A string of hits is to follow.

Suddenly, miraculously, and with mystifying ease, he is back with the world at his feet.

It is instant hysteria.

Date: 3 December, 1968. A sensual, black-clad Elvis in the NBC-TV Special that resurrected him. The King has returned.

5

"Elvis Presley remains the quintessential American pop star: gaudy, garish, compromised in his middle age by commercial considerations, yet gifted with an enormous talent and a charismatic appeal beyond mere nostalgia. Presley remains a true American artist – one of the greatest in American popular music, a singer of native brilliance and a performer of magnetic dimensions."
– Jim Miller, Rolling Stone

For his first public appearance after eight years in seclusion, Elvis goes to Nevada, to those diamonds in the desert, to Las Vegas, the first genuine lunar base. A city of dreams, built from plastic and neon, it casts phosphorescent messages over the wilderness desolation, is a jewel of cold electric fire burning bright in the night. An Aladdin's cave of the American subconscious, both promise and prison to all who would enter, it is, to be sure, the one place on earth in which a legend can reignite its own image.

Here, with the machines, with the blackjack and baccarat, with the dealers and the hookers and the criminal and the insane, in the glitter and timelessness (no clocks, no windows, no day or night), he will resurrect an American myth. The rock will be a parody of what has gone before, a sublimely self-mocking resumé of his own great achievements; but it will, in its humour and its superb presentation, give back the old excitement to the watcher: he knows just what he's doing.

The white columns soar upward through the dark humid air, encircling a metallic globe, surrounded by flags, dominated by the huge boards that hurl out towards the Strip the message that Elvis is back, his face multiplied. And the lights on these boards form a glaring fluorescence, a staggering

orange, an ever-changing yellow and crimson that dazzles the eyes. And the sum of the whole, in all its architectural arrogance, is like a launching tower built on the moon, hypnotising the multitudes.

The myth looks even better than he ever looked before, coming on with trumpets and drums and guitars, to an explosion of flash-bulbs and hysteria. Now the audience is predominantly middle class and middle-aged, no longer rebellious but playing the system, safe in their money, in their own ideas of purity, finally arrived, in the year of 1969, to let nostalgia fill them and lay them waste. And there, on the stage, stands the highlight of their lives returned to flesh and blood, rising up from the tomb. One hell of a man, truly tall, dark and handsome, he sports a black Karate suit, a wicked grin and bushy sideburns; he is pure and untrammelled *machismo* hunched over a guitar.

A wave of nostalgia for the fifties has been sweeping the country. Whether or not this has encouraged Elvis back, it certainly does nothing to harm him. No, rather he plays on it, on his knowledge of his own history, and so turns his first season in the showroom of the International into a classic revival in every sense.

He kicks off with "Blue Suede Shoes", charges through "I Got A Woman", then leans over the mike in that old seductive pose and starts growling from the back of his throat, a sly, honeyed come-on. They may be middle-aged, have cropped hair and bouffants, but they are out of their seats like teenagers and the applause is enough to shake the stage. So he rocks the mike gently, hums and growls, fools a little, than lets rip with a fast "All Shook Up", his legs jolting like pistons. A decade disappears, they are back where they started, and as he spreads wide his legs and rakes the mike across his body, he comes over much stronger than any reality they might yet have known.

He understands this very well – and he knows his own age. So he works along the safe lines of instant nostalgia, but he does so with a style and panache that come close to pure magic. Lithe, raunchy, the sweat pouring down his face, he now moves with the precision of an athlete, the grace of a dancer. His movements, in fact, no longer seen uncontrolled, but instead are stylised, immaculately choreographed, and resplendent with high visual dramatics.

He throws in Chuck Berry, and Leiber and Stoller, and Carl Perkins, and he re-works the Sun songs, some old ballads, some new, each building on the last, each beautifully controlled, hips swaying, hands chopping, his teeth and eyes flashing, held in the spotlights, surrealistic in the strobes, sometimes falling to his knees, sometimes frozen in brief silence in controlled karate poses that turn him obliquely into something much more than he is: a figure in a ballet, now

Date: 31 July, 1969. Location: International Hotel in Las Vegas. Elvis's come-back performance was a triumph in every sense. These photos recapture the exitement.

poised for a pirouette, now imitating a *pas de deux*, unreal, unearthly, a black dream of pure motion – Nureyev in a jumpsuit, no less.

It is no exaggeration. Of all the rock singers who have aged with the times he is the only one who has kept his sense of grace. Flamboyant and flashy, sexy and self-mocking, he works with the instincts of a genius to give poetry to the basic rock performance. Thus he spirals around, his hand sweeping through the spotlight, and falls down to one knee, his head back, a fist clenched, and is frozen for an instant in a thin blade of silver. And he rises up slowly, curving snakelike, hypnotic, while the violins soar to new heights of cliché, which surrender before him. Then the drums thunder out, a guitar whips the silence, and he is suddenly moving, his groin swinging, head jerking, a diamond-studded fist swathing through the hot air like the whip that will bring the band home, cracking on towards the climax.

There is nothing remotely real about this performer: he has lived with us too long. Now he is a legend who will charge the adrenalin merely by the fact that he is *there*. But he's good, and he knows it, and will offer it leaving nothing to chance. He leans across his guitar, strokes its flanks, croons above it, grins wickedly and rolls his head slightly: we are back in the fifties. Yes, and he even repeats his little speech before ''Hound Dog'', a brief, rambling monologue, quite senseless, great fun, that mint 'n' julep voice coming out of the speakers like the ghost of a lover in the cold sheets, just playing with memories . . .

''When I, ah . . . when I tried to think of a special song for tonight . . . huh, huh, huh . . . ah . . . special song that really says something, if you know . . . ah . . . a *message* song . . . I, ah . . . ah . . . I, ah . . . What'd I do? Oh yeah! I came up with this . . . I looked her square in the eye . . . because that's all she had . . . this one big square eye in the middle of her . . . ah . . .

I said, Baby . . . huh, huh, huh . . . she was weird too, you know, she . . . ah . . . huh, huh . . . I got real close up to her, and it was a very tender, touching moment . . . ah . . . and I said:

"You ain't nothin' but a hound dog!"

And they're out of their seats as the years roll away, as the snap of the drums and the savage guitars cut a path through the decade he wasted. It's a much faster version, more contemporary, less exciting, but the delivery weighs nothing against the sentiment. Now, as he moves, as his lean face pours sweat, it's impossible even to think of the bloated buffoon who wasted eight of his years in bum movies. (Did they ever, in truth, really exist? Did he really live in that vacuum, in the dark rooms of Graceland, nameless, like a man without a face?) Whatever ghost he has exorcised, whatever fear he now destroys, he is performing like a slave released from chains, like a man with a hunger. So he lets go the guitar,

133

Above: Mixing with the fans after the 1969 come-back.
Opposite: Rehearsals for the second bout at Las Vegas.

slaps one hand on a thigh, then starts swinging his fist at the group like a demon unleashed. It's a circular movement, syncopated to his hips, and it takes us right back, through the years of oblivion, to the days when he shocked the whole world, when he seemed like a monster. But now, as he does it, he is grinning, self-mocking, and the movements are seen to be a choreographed gesture towards those roots that are now far behind him: he recreates his own history.

These first Vegas performances are masterfully controlled · tributes to that past which has made him what he is. In the sense that he is out to recapture the faithful, he is working to very fine rules. Thus he runs through his hits, begs their tears with his ballads, and climaxes with a very lengthy version of his latest big smash. It is not an accident that this song, "Suspicious Minds", is a mixture of the old and the new, a supercharged rhythmic ballad. For indeed they are ballads that this gentleman prefers, and he offers them up with the sort of emotion that his rock songs can no longer have. "Suspicious Minds" is a bridge song, a fine mingling of both, and before its surging rhythm and some spiralling vocal harmonies, he uses his baritone and his trembling vibrato to pour into it all the emotion he can muster. Then, in the middle of· it, he drops to one knee, clenches a fist, and with head bowed takes a gospel-like break, linking up all the influences. He is crouched over, worshipping, transfixed in the spotlight, and his voice warbles and groans, and comes out like an anthem, against nothing but the audience, the band almost silent, and then – "Yeah! Yeah! *Yeah*! YEAH!" – and *bam*! the band is back, the music piles high, and he rises like a black snake from the dark of its lair and starts shaking his torso to the rhythm, socking it to them. The song is a pile-driver, over six minutes long, and he slides across the stage, legs bent back and outstretched, spine curved with the mike held above him – then springs up, his hair flying, never missing a note, leading into the multiple finale . . . "*Well don't ya know*"/BAM! BAM!/"*We're caught in a trap*" (fist swinging, hips rocking) /BAM! BAM!/"*Ah can't walk out*" (legs stabbing, heels pounding) /"*because I love you so much, Babe-ay-ay-ayay* . . ." Then takes it down to a silence, and then builds it up again, takes it down, builds it up, repeats it once more, then starts kicking across the stage, high kicks, fast and vicious, athletically, beautifully, karate-chopping through the strobe lights in a blur of pure motion, until he climaxes with a shimmy, a good old-fashioned shake, and then drops to one knee, head bowed and arms outstretched, and is finally, and most grace-fully, finished.

A way-out performance.

These shows are masterly, but they also are tied to a past he no longer seems to want. They have given him confidence, put him back where he was but now he will follow his own desires. Thus, six months later, when he returns to the International for the second time, he reduces the golden oldies to jokes, works out some new material. He is now usually all in white, either sequinned or tasseled, the stiff collar turned up over lean, shadowed cheeks, the lopsided grin mischievous, his eyes glittering with mirth, one cool lover, one conquerer, one walking dream. And though there is a confidence that borders on arrogance, his sly, self-mocking humour will assuage it. And his grasp on the choreography of pop is now even more controlled and impressive: he explodes out of stillness.

Las Vegas is cabaret land, a club room, and he knows where he's at. He is smooth, sleek, witty and wicked, a more God-like Dean Martin, a rough-rocking Sinatra, an unreachable legend dressed in light-reflecting white, stepping forth to prostrate his waiting flock, the backdrops a rich imagery. True, there is a rock group (and a good one it is), but the orchestra is massive, there are *two* vocal groups, and even the back-up musicians sing harmony – one huge sound, one spectacle. And he does, to be sure, put on a show, he hypnotises his audience. It's a well-rehearsed routine of almost operatic ballads and some sophisticated, theatrical rock: it is some-thing for everyone.

He opens with a modern version of "See See Rider Blues", and it is fast and vicious and precise. The girls swoop in behind him, pumping out a gospel sound, and the group plays a mean, rocking rhythm. But the brass is going mad, working hard to pin it down to the level of a cabaret opener – the conductor's hands wave. Still, it works, it's a hard, raunchy assault; it's a bit of fair rock, whipping up the nostalgia, and it leaves room for play in other fields, prepares the new ground. So he launches into "Release Me", bounds through "Sweet Caroline" and then moves pretty fast into ballads, the real heavy production jobs. He does "Mary in the Morning"

This page: Winding up rehearsals in the M-G-M studios.
Opposite and overleaf: Las Vegas, August, 1970.

and "Bridge Over Troubled Water", and the performance is superb. His body quivers in spasms, his head rolls on his shoulders, he clenches his fists and lets the sweat pour down his face, and when he gets to "I've Lost You" he is down on his knees as if death is the only alternative: the tears streak their mascara.

Yes, sir, it is brilliant. It is also sincere. And if he's guilty of many things, he's not guilty of slacking when it comes to giving value for money: he does not disappoint. And if the rockers are fewer, they are also more spectacular, laid out with the panache and sense of dynamics that turn modest numbers into ball-biters, into visual fireworks. Thus in "Polk Salad Annie", which is one of his best, he starts off with a monologue, slides into the song, starts winding up the girls, shuts them down, turns them on, and then whips up the band with that famous swinging fist, with those extraordinary gyrations – all Mick Jagger violence and Nureyev grace at once – and finally finishes as a blur of pure motion in strobe lights, a white-dazzle hallucination, and comes out of it all looking drenched, the grin arrogant, sublime.

The monologue itself is a masterpiece of timing, slurred, honey-toned, sometimes mocking, always sensual, each sly word fitted in to the snap of the drums, the walk Southern and lazy, a Dean Martin pastiche, and then – *whap! whap!* – to the drums, his hand slapping his thigh, before spiralling and slipping smoothly in with the rhythm, singing, "*Down in Louisiana . . . where the alligators grow so mean . . .*" and he is

that alligator, and you are right down there, and then he whips it all up and the stage is pure frenzy, and there's nothing in your eyes but this gyrating heathen, this hypnotic blur in the craze of the lights, and the sound rapes your ears and the flashing blinds your eyes – and then suddenly, shocked silence, it is over, he is frozen, one white God.

Did he ever go through all those movies with no sweat on his painted brow? Impossible to believe that this theatrical wizard ever let himself do what he did, didn't go quite insane. Even more impossible – as he pirouettes to catch the mike, as he slides across the stage, as he rises like a dream in slow motion and crimson light, as his hand curves through that thin blade of silver, falling lazily, outstretched – impossible to believe, as he does this and more, that he would ever let himself slip again.

And yet the echoes of his former career are now ominously present. Already, after one season of highly successful rock, he is returning to the realms of middle-road show biz. Of course he can do it – no one doubts that he can – but then no one understands why he would want to.

There is a sweet old cliché called the Trap of Success, and it is possible that even Elvis can't escape it. A consummate artist, he is cornered by his own image, by the breadth of his audience, by the size of his fame, by the mystique of his own presence, by financial considerations, by his age, and by the cold fact that most rockers lose their dignity in the end. The permutations make mountains, building higher each year, and as he squats on the top, growing loftier by the minute, he is bound by necessity to move away from what he is into areas of even broader acceptance.

Yes, over the years he's sung every conceivable kind of song in an attempt to catch all of the market; now, when he is back, when the world is at his feet, he will find that the audience he made for himself will demand what he gave them through their lives – a little rock, a little blues, a little country, a little gospel, plus pastiche Hawaiian ballads, some Neopolitan and operatic chanters, with a few sophisticated swingers thrown in (most particularly in Vegas). The audience is vast and its appetite is huge; thus the voice that can feed it must suffer. He does it very well – no one else could quite manage

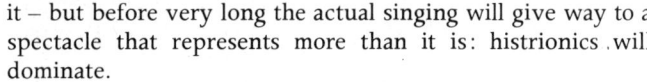

it – but before very long the actual singing will give way to a spectacle that represents more than it is: histrionics will dominate.

Then, of course, there is the narcissism, that intriguing self-absorption, that sublime vice which gave him universal appeal and yet finally locked him up in himself, surrounded by mirrors. He still lives with his "ol' boys", with the voices of his childhood, and even now at the height of his resurgence he's removed from the outer world. So he doesn't return to Memphis, he starts making sloppy records, he travels in the glass cage of his own God-like stature; as he must, he slips back into a parody of his own quite remarkable achievements. And it doesn't take long.

Yet no matter his carelessness, his indifference to criticism, his insistence upon working with his old friends and cousins, he is stunning when he walks on a stage. For this reason there is no comparison between the records he's putting out and the performances he gives in the flesh. Elvis "live" is superb.

Part of the American consciousness, he now tours the country that made him. From 1970 to 1973 he is swinging high. He goes to Phoenix and Detroit, to Albuquerque and Little Rock, to Houston and Miami, to San Francisco, Los Angeles, San Diego and Denver, to Oakland and Portland and

Seattle, to Madison Square Garden, New York. He travels by private jet, flying in to enormous crowds, looking garish and diamond-studded, his eyes hidden by huge glasses, his bulky figure surrounded by bodyguards, by gleaming black limousines. And he greets all the people and accepts the city's keys, and is rushed away to hide in hotel suites, to rest before chaos. Though now he is indifferent to the studios, though he makes his records too quickly; if his sales are already dropping and the movies are dead – no sweat. In the flesh he is monstrous, a total sell-out – and he seems to be captured by the contact.

His flash clothes are even flashier, his arrogance is stupendous, and his theme tune is ''Thus Spake Zarathustra'' – the World-Riddle Theme, the God Theme. No one else could get away with it (though others will imitate it), and the sound of that introduction will send shivers down the spine as the spotlights wander over the stage, as the tympany thunders. Such a tune conjurs up all the mystery of the universe, and to many in the void of their own lives, this myth on the stage is just that. Thus the band tails ''Zarathustra'' with a fierce, driving rhythm, an apocalyptic sound, and the legend bounds on, a flash of white with a gold cape, studs glittering, tassels flying, and hits the mike like the Man on the Mount.

He burns through ''See See Rider'' or ''That's All Right Mama'', leaning forward on one foot, braced lightly on the other, the guitar slanted upward, a mere prop that he plays with, fingers snapping or curled round the mike, which he sometimes nearly swallows. His body is pneumatic, almost drilling through the boards, exploding with tension and contained rhythmic drive as he swivels on one foot, points a finger to the side, and then falls into a crouch as the guitarist takes a solo, grinning wickedly, punching upward with his own guitar, not playing, just fooling. It's a moment of self-mockery, a pure recall to the fifties, and as the applause explodes over him he returns casually to the mike, shrugging, close to giggling, then takes hold and rocks it roughly before howling back into the song, his eyes closed, left leg shaking.

And then, as he finishes, as the trumpets kill it off, the guitar punches back and forth, in a blur, with blinding speed, and he is taking his bow before the last note is hit – while the guitar is sent spinning like a missile through the spotlight to the hands of a lackey behind him.

It's a gas of an opener, but before thay can recover he's already well into the second song. The brass is staccato, the rhythm section punches out, and as lovely Ronnie Tutt takes a dive bomb on the drums, Elvis stretches out his right hand, an aeroplane's wing, and then sweeps in a perfect circle, crouched low and taut, and comes up with legs parted, the mike to his lips, and is into ''Proud Mary'' with a vengeance. Not stupendous on record, it makes stupendous viewing as he gyrates his hips, karate-chops across the stage, kicks his legs and then starts swinging that right fist, teeth gritted, sweat pouring. ''*Rollin' . . . rollin' . . . rollin' down the river . . .*'' And he rolls and punches forwards and stabs the air with his feet, and then carries it on home to a grand Kung Fu climax.

His greatest gift to pop is his air of the untouchable combined with the illusion of intimacy. The most remote star in history, he nevertheless manages to reduce a massive audience to mere Family. Thus he wanders across the stage, through a flood of golden light, and makes small jokes that could only be personal. He unzips his jumpsuit, fiddles distractedly with his belt, wipes the sweat from his face with a scarf and throws it out to a lady. ''Lawd have mercy'', he says in that most Southern of honeyed drawls. ''I'm outa mah mind, I'm outa mah body, I'm jest goin' *crazy* up here!'' And then starts singing ''Love Me'', wandering lazily back and forth, leaning down to kiss the girls, accepting gifts, giving scarves – pure primal show business – and cooing with sly mockery as some lady grabs his leg, ''Oh, honey-chile, I ain't what *you* think I am.'' It is narcissism and self-awareness neatly embraced: the saint and the sinner, the romantic lover and the stud, the little boy who came out of the backwoods and the legend he now is. ''Good evening, ladies and gentlemen . . . I mean, *afternoon,* ladies and . . . or *night* or whatever . . . Hey, man, what show *are* we doin' today? Just *where* are we, man?'' And then goes ''*Whoops!*'' and shakes his head in mock bewilderment, and murmurs, ''I think we better stop right this minute, folks. Howyaall? Nice to see ya.'' And even as he's saying this, the bass begins to throb, a deep, hypnotic chant, and you can see that left leg moving, first twitching, then shaking, then the fingers start snapping, very casual, quite precise, and then *chop!* go the guitars, and *slap!* goes the hip, and then the girls begin to clap, a sharp, staccato rhythm, and then the small talk is a monologue and then the monologue is a song and then *whap! whap!* and he's off, into ''Polk Salad Annie'', and he's riding her good, bearing down heavy on her, singing meanly, ''*Yah know what I* mean *now* . . .'' Of which there can be no doubt.

Elvis is presented as a man with superhuman attributes, yet he always contradicts this very stance. This contradiction in itself is what makes him magnetic, since enigmas are the roots of obsession. He is dressed like a prince, the diamonds glitter, the cape waves; he is tall and athletic, and in the cunning play of lights (all that pale blue and crimson) he seems as unreal as the ghost of a Greek god, the original perfect male. Who cares if he's made up? if the lights are deceiving? if the tune of ''Thus Spake Zarathustra'' makes you fall for the trick? The fact remains that he *is*, that he floats through countless dreams, and that whatever he was, or wherever he is going, he is now, at this moment, the living symbol of freedom and light. Yes, it is all too much – he has been with us too long – by all the laws of our logic he should find it impossible to descend from this. And yet he does – or he weaves this fine illusion; he stands up before thousands and he draws them all to him, and the sly-

ness is in the silk of his talk, in his wit, in his self-effacement. Supernatural are the surroundings – the dazzling lights, the drowning colours, the glittering orchestra and the bright group and the sexy girls, the mean man himself in his jewelled suit – but he gets down there amongst them, takes their hands, drops them kisses, is insinuating and sincere and sometimes violent: he takes no shit from anyone. Yes, one minute grinning, like a schoolboy, like a stud, the next he will turn on some loudmouth beside him and the tone of his voice is pure venom: ''Just cool it, man! *Cool it!*'' It is true. He does this. And whether genuine or staged, it encourages cold chills, makes the flesh creep. Will he actually *do* it. Will he *smash* that guy? And then, before it happens, he has shrugged and turned away, perhaps hitching up the belt, grinning lopsided and self-mocking, saying cheerfully, ''Oh, boy! There's some *folk* out there!'' It's either unblushing showmanship or genuine emotion, but whatever, it works, makes him fascinating. You forget ''Zarathustra'' and the spectacular backdrops, and you think, Christ, the guy's just like *me* – he is human, he *feels* things. It's cool, it's even *natural*, and you can't help but believe it when he looks at one of his group, shakes his head and grins ruefully, then murmurs, ''Lord, man, I just *dread* this whole thing.'' The band plays. He starts singing.

He sings the ballads as if he's standing in church, as if he's back beside his folk, back in time, back in memories, as if he's suddenly lost sight of where he is. He usually sings them with eyes closed, head back, one fist clenched, a foot tapping, hips swaying abstractedly. The voice is now deeper, more mature, quite immaculate, and it floats upon a tide of true emotion, sometimes quivering, not lying. It is, without embarrassment, and with a quite guileless intimacy, a voice that conveys real

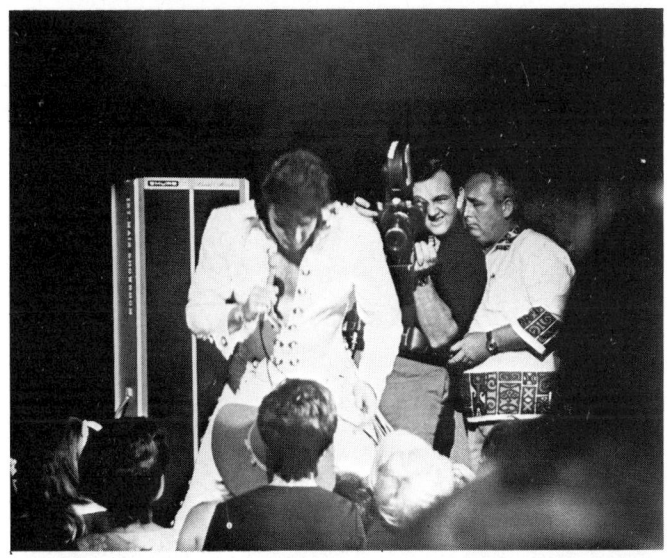

loss and grief. It is also, beyond doubt, quite instinctively and nakedly, a voice of the most romantic sensuality. If he sings of the spirit, he imbues it with the flesh; if he sings of desire he speaks of love. *"Who will I find to lie beside me?"* he sings, and the words, which are simple, which are quite simply desolate, are filled with the tragedy, with the crystalline grief, of a flesh that might never be touched. *"Leaving me lonely,"* he adds, and the last word is a killer, a knife through all hope, a common word transformed to pure poetry by its tone of delivery: an anthem, a hymn.

It is indeed the hymnal quality of his delivery that transforms the most mundane offerings into miniature classics. Just as during his film period his better ballads were ignored, so now, as he tours, as he lays waste to America, he will fight against a barrage of criticism for deserting rock music. And it is true that during 1973 he slows down, starts reducing the temperature, and seemingly oblivious to the cries of the be-

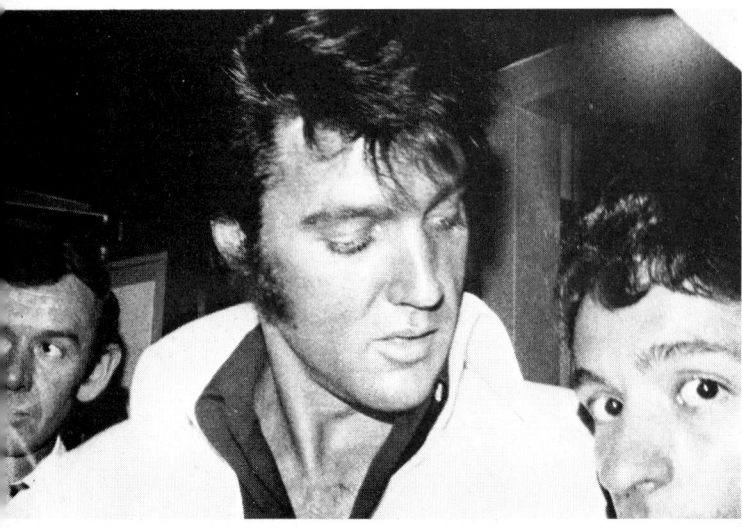

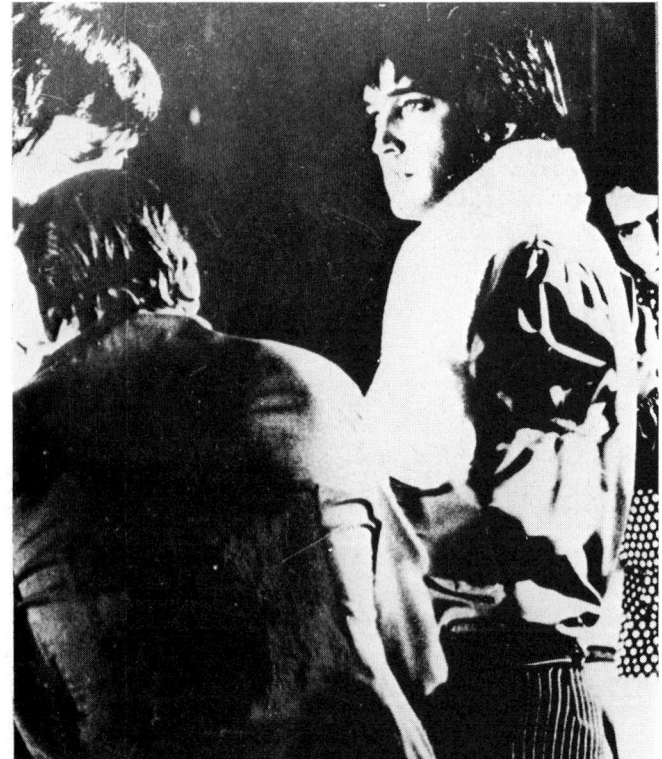

trayed, insists on building up his repertoire of ballads.

Possibly he does this because he knows that he is aging, that he's now reaching forty, that sooner or later he must forget the past, leave the young man behind, and build up a new kind of audience. If this be true, then it shows astute thinking, a firm grasp on what he is and where he must go. And no matter the reason, small difference in the choice, he is doing whatever he is drawn to, and doing it well. Ballads they may be, but the delivery is beautiful, a very rare combination of pure vocal pyrotechnics and superbly delivered histrionics: he comes across like an actor.

Las Vegas becomes a stint as regular as the movies – but at least he starts touring America. The only films during this time are two documentaries: Elvis, That's The Way It Is *(1971) and* Elvis On Tour *(1973). Both films show Elvis on stage and at rehearsals; both are disappointing.*

It is said that most good singers are by nature good actors, and certainly in Presley's case this is true. Most actors work best when they are faced with an audience, when they can feel the response, and this too applies to him. If his years in the movies nearly murdered his talent, if they threatened to crush him beneath the weight of their anonymity, he now proves that he has much fight left in him. Yes, he sings like an actor, he acts out the words, his face is a mirror to the emotions he conveys and his hands which are large, diamond-studded and yet delicate weave hypnotic arabesques in the spotlights.

His eyes close. His head turns slightly sideways. He seems to fall asleep above the mike in his hand, gently swaying, just hanging loose. The stage lights dim. A mist of lavender emanates. The orchestra is silhouetted in a backwash of pale blue, like those figures we view in our dreams, never moving, just present. And now seen from the chest up, the white jumpsuit dazzling his Adonis face highlighted and close to unreal, he becomes a kind of strange, abstract vision – it's pure cinema, a fantasy world. And just as you forget where you are, who you're watching, the music floats in and he is singing.

"*When you're weary/Feeling small/When tears are in your eyes/I will dry them all . . .*" And he's leaning slightly forward, braced on one foot, breathing over the mike like a man above his mistress, his free hand before him, gently weaving in the air, suddenly quite delicate, an Oriental girl's dance, a story in mime, the fingers floating in space between the song's painful words, conveying more than the words themselves could ever do. "*I'll take your hand*", he sings, clenching his fist, bringing it to his forehead, a pure Brando gesture as the spotlight thins down and leaves blackness on all but his face: one face floating, a lover's dream. And his voice at this moment is a thing of pure nobility, hovering in silence, isolated in stillness, before rising operatically, coming out in full force against the brass and the violins and the vocal groups: "*Like a bridge over troubled water/I will lay me down . . .*" And his spine curves impossibly, his head falls right back, and as the spotlight widens and the stagelights blaze forth, he is curved like a bow, like

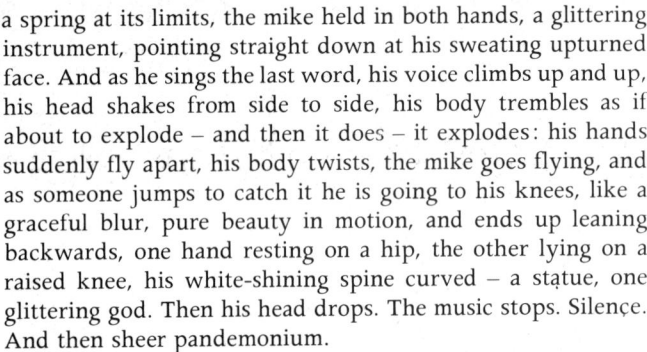

a spring at its limits, the mike held in both hands, a glittering instrument, pointing straight down at his sweating upturned face. And as he sings the last word, his voice climbs up and up, his head shakes from side to side, his body trembles as if about to explode – and then it does – it explodes: his hands suddenly fly apart, his body twists, the mike goes flying, and as someone jumps to catch it he is going to his knees, like a graceful blur, pure beauty in motion, and ends up leaning backwards, one hand resting on a hip, the other lying on a raised knee, his white-shining spine curved – a statue, one glittering god. Then his head drops. The music stops. Silence. And then sheer pandemonium.

It is acting, most assuredly, and of a very high order; it is in fact the new form of theatre. He will take his audience and he will convey to them emotion in a manner more direct than any other. And like the good actor he is, he will constantly surprise them, will keep slipping and sliding through a variety of moods with the guile of a salamandar in the flame. So before they can breathe, before the tears dry from their eyes, he says, "Oh, boy! A good 'un! Just laid us out!" And he waves to the guitarist, and a wah-wah tears the air, and he shrieks, kicks the air, and then drops down very low, and then gives us his new brand of fireworks: karate to rock music.

It's graceful, athletic, modestly exciting, and it probably marks the end of an era, the final fling of The Pelvis. He will put on a show, and he will make sure it's good, but he's taken his measure and he knows his own age, and no matter what they say he'll leave rock behind. The new Elvis Presley is in the beautiful "I'm Leavin'", in the rhythmic "Let Me Be There", in his exquisitely acted version of "Softly, As I Leave You", in "Why Me Lord" and "Help Me"; in the superb "Loving Arms" and, most of all, in "American Trilogy". This is where he now stands.

As a performer, Elvis Presley has never left America, and it's now very doubtful that he will. Just as his isolation enshrined him in his own past, so his indefinable lack of volition has enslaved him to his own country. It has been suggested and is very likely true, that he now views himself as a particularly American phenomenon and can scarcely conceive of anything beyond. He's religious, patriotic, totally steeped in his own music and possibly, in private, just as rural now as he was when a boy back in Tupelo. The myths of America

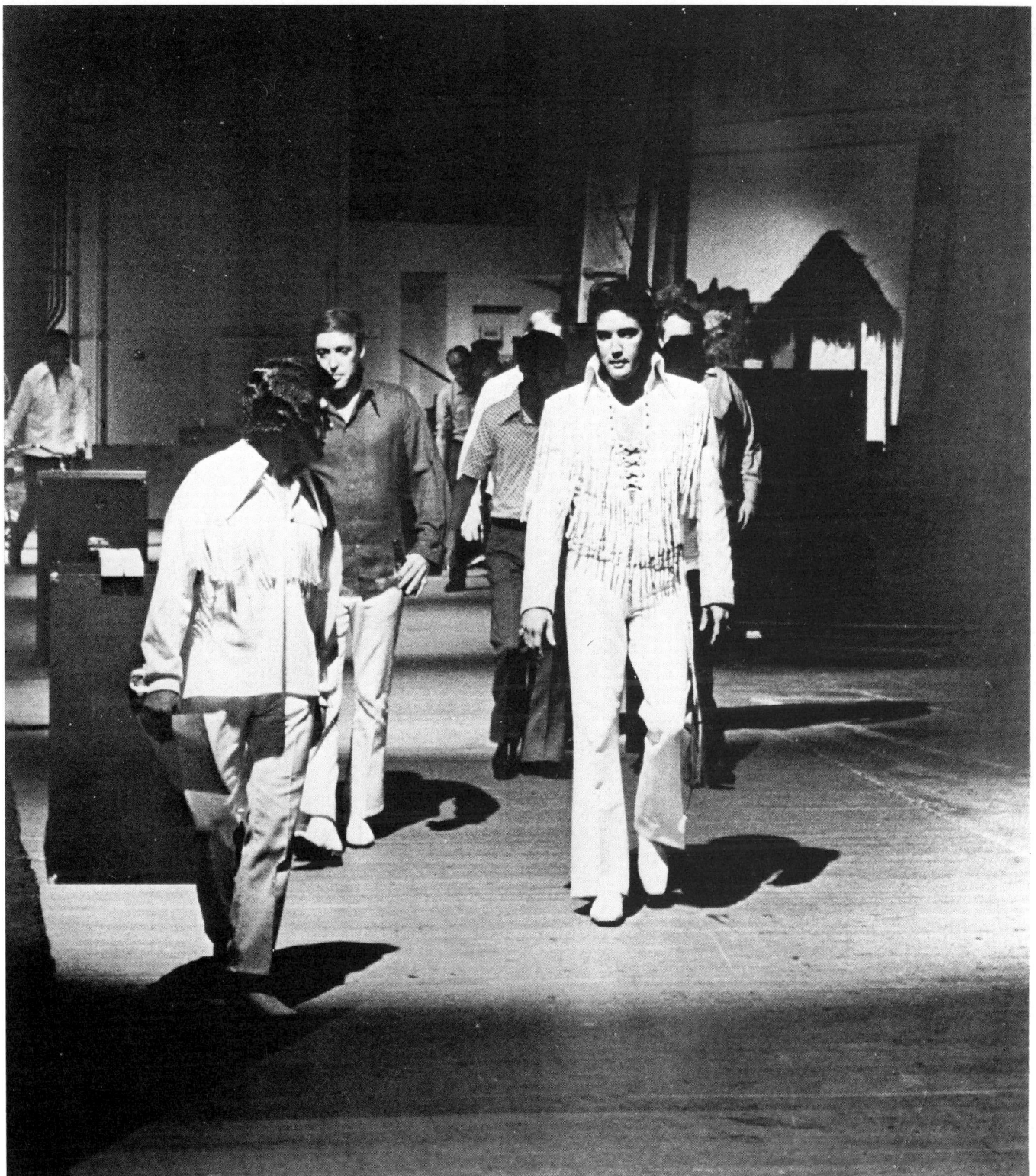

lie behind him; they nurtured him; they protect him. Now reaching middle age, impaled on the pinnacle with half his life to live but no new heights to be scaled, he might well be drawing closer – if closer he can get – to the friends and the memories and the emotions of his past, to whatever is most familiar and unchanging. If this be true, it could account for his increasing love of gospel music, country songs and American audiences. Certainly only Elvis could sing gospel at Las Vegas – and certainly Elvis's treatment of "American Trilogy" (now

almost his anthem) is an eloquent testimony to where he stands.

He recently sang it in Memphis.

The stage lights dim – dim almost to total darkness – and Elvis walks to his man, has a quick drink of water, then turns around to be fitted with the gold-lined cape. He then walks back to the mike, a spotlight covers his face, and he takes the mike off the stand and bows his head. He turns slightly sideways, and in this moment of silence the reverence is enough to move mountains. Then, most gently, as if offering the tablets, Elvis simply raises his free hand and points.

The treat now begins.

To an acoustic guitar and almost imperceptible back-up vocal, Elvis Presley, dressed in diamonds and emeralds and gold, mournfully (and immaculately) croons: *"Oh I wish I were/In the Land of Cotton/Old folks there/ Are not forgotten . . ."* And now raising his head slightly, his gaze cast afar, one hand high and glittering in the spotlight: *"Look away/ Look away/ Look away/Dixieland . . ."*

A few bars on the guitar and Elvis steps out of the spotlight, and with a choke in his voice murmurs, "Sing it, fellas." Another light falls on the Stamps, a very gospel-sounding group, and Elvis, in the shadows, now stands with head bowed, as they sing, as if in church: *"Oh I wish I was in Dixie/ Away/Away . . . In Dixieland I'd make my stand/To live and die for Dixie . . ."*

Now Elvis steps back into the spotlight, and his head is still bowed, one hand clasped in the other, the mike close to his lips, singing: *"For Dixieland/That's where I was born/ Early, Lord, one frosty morn . . ."* And they're all there with him, travelling back that thirty years, back to the cottonfields, to the poor boy of the South, to where the myths of America are nurtured and heroes are born . . . *"Look away/Look away/ Look away/Dixieland . . ."*

And on the last word Ronnie Tutt plays a march on the snare drum, and Elvis starts quivering, lifting high his proud head, the mike tight in both hands, staring up at the heavens, singing, "*Glory, glory, Hallelujah!*" Drawing out and warbling on the word "Hallelujah" until – BAM! BAM! BAM! – the brass (now stage-lit) and the violins (now stage-lit) and *three* vocal groups (now stage-lit) join in: "*Glory, glory, Hallelujah/ Glory, glory, Hallelujah/And His truth goes marching on . . .*"

Then the stage lights die out again as the orchestra fades

Elvis adds a gold-lined cape to his increasingly colourful jump suits. Top left: Charlie Hodge encourages Elvis on guitar while the taciturn Jerry Scheff supports on bass. Overleaf: The many moods of The King on stage.

away, leaving only one spot-light, burning down like a beacon – on Elvis.

He is sweating and tense, holding tight to the mike ... His head rolls back on his shoulders, his eyes close; he listens. A lonely guitar plucks out some sad chords ... And now Elvis leans over, almost eating the mike, visibly trembling with emotion, and magically, most mysteriously, making the most banal words suddenly resonant with the sound of pure faith: *"So hush little baby/Don't you cry/You know your daddy's/bound to die ..."* And now a lonely flute comes in, and a quiet vocal group, as Elvis, almost talking, his voice hushed and superb, intones: *"But all my trials, Lord/Will soon be over ..."* And now, yes, they see it, all the distance he has travelled, from a common heritage, into their dreams, sharing their destiny, their history: they reach out towards him. And he, knowing this, turns his back to the audience, bows his head, lifts his head, rocks back on his heels, a tall silhouette, just out of the spotlight, enamoured by the lone trill of the flute, almost tragically stricken ...

150

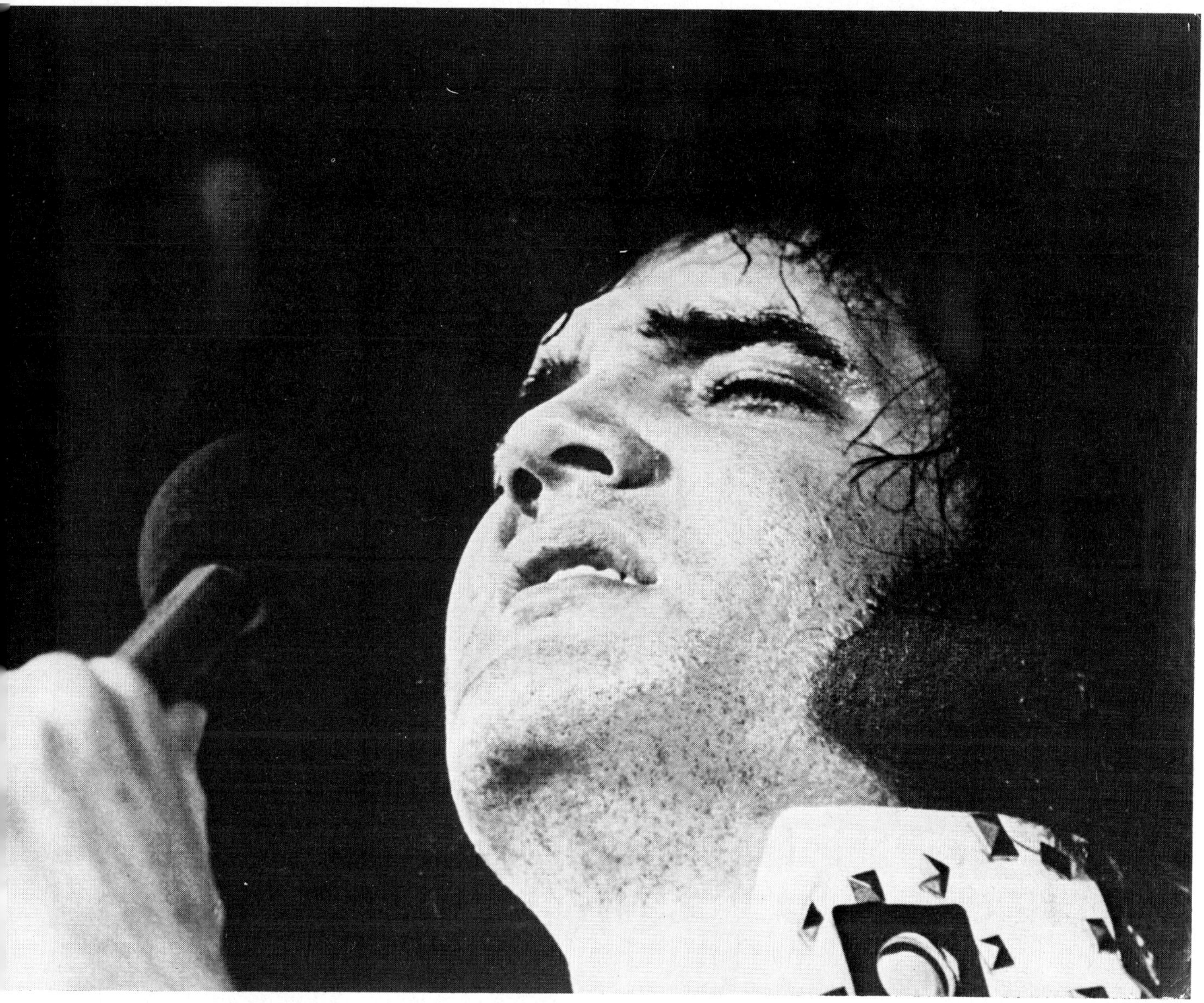

Then the drums begin to thunder, the full orchestra winds up, the three vocal groups combined sound like a choir in a cathedral, and the strobe lights start flashing; the sound builds and builds, reaches deafening proportions, and the stage lights pour down as Elvis slowly turns around, one hand on the mike, the other holding out the gold cape – yes, pure gold, and it shimmers and flashes, one half of a beautiful sun climbing over the horizon – and then – BAM! BAM! BAM! – Elvis's fist punches three times, the whole stage explodes, and then, sudden crescendo, his right hand above his head, the incredible gold cape waving, a pure clarion call, and they're into the symphonic finale: *"Glory, glory, Hallelujah/Glory, glory, Hallelujah/Glory, glory, Hallelujah/And His truth goes marching on . . ."* And as the last word builds – and builds and builds – the stage lights come on full blast, the whole orchestra

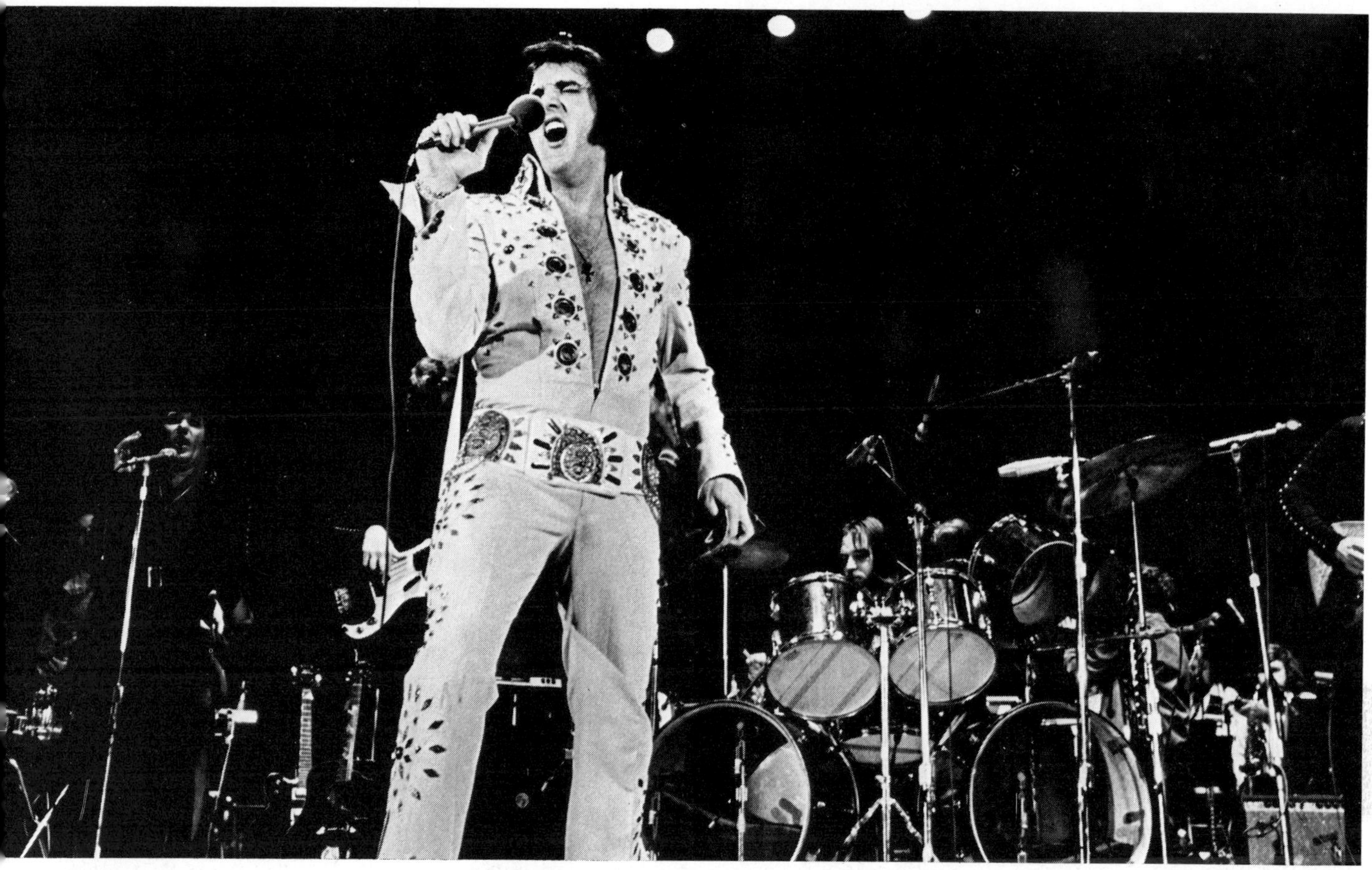

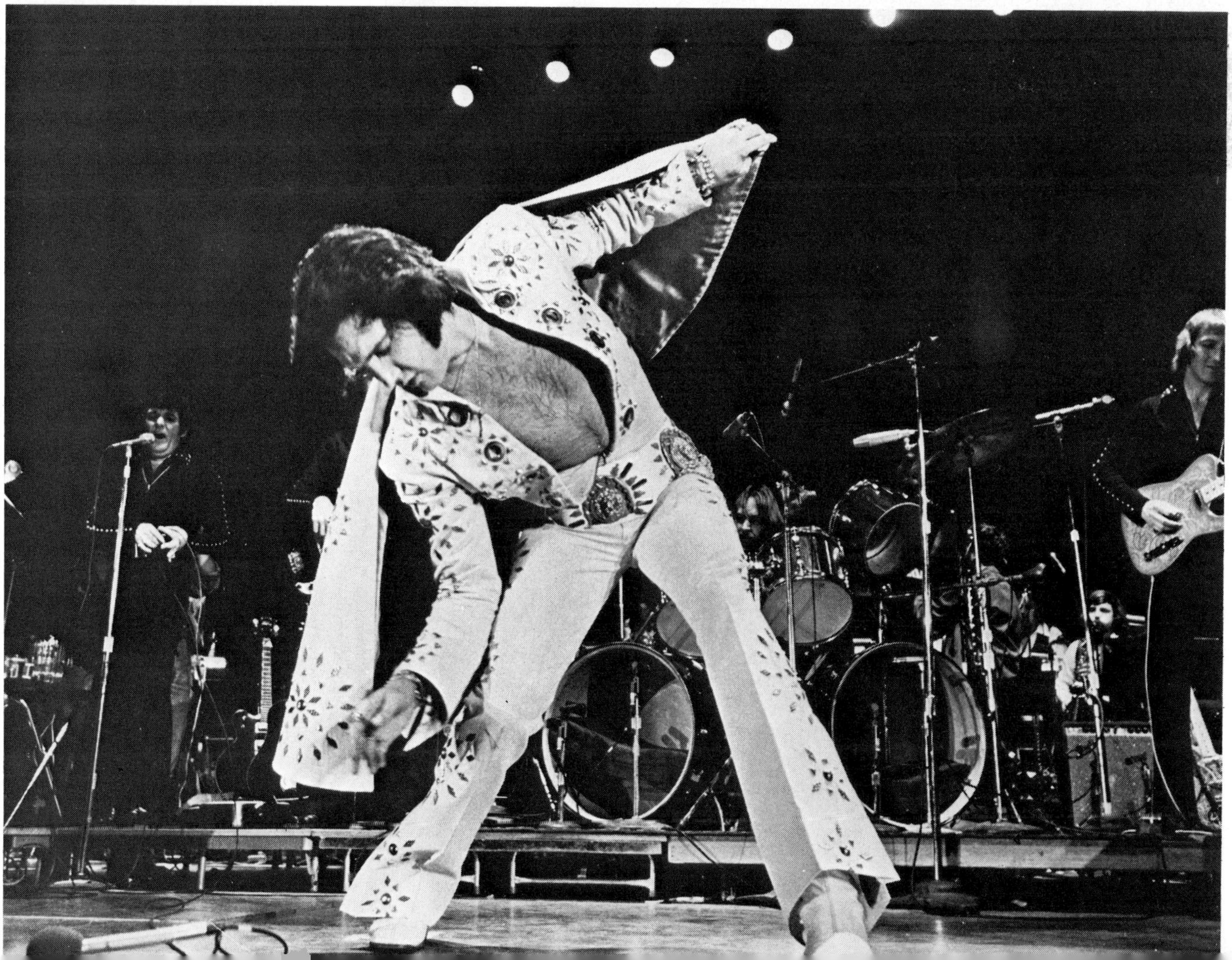

is standing, and there, behind the band, stretching over the huge wall, lights flashing all over it like the silver birds of truth, is an enormous and most garish Stars and Stripes . . . *"And His truth goes marching on . . ."* BAM! BAM! BAM! BAAM! BAAAAMMMMMMMM! And Elvis stands with legs parted, his head bowed, his arms outstretched, and the lovely gold cape is a huge sun, burning up the whole audience. So they rise to their feet, their tears flow, their hands clap, and he falls to one knee, bows his head, crosses arms, and wraps the gold cape around him like a shroud.

The lights dim. He is hidden.

High camp, superb theatre – call it what you will – it represents some kind of extraordinary grasp on the psychology of a captive audience. He knows what he symbolises, and what he is and where he stands, and he will take his own history and wrap it in mythology and serve it up as the truth everlasting, the impossible dream. He has come out of poverty and the child's clinging fears to a world in which reality won't impinge; he will not let this go. And so he takes what he has gleaned, every trick, every instinct, and he uses it to keep himself on top of the mountain, regardless of what price must be paid. No longer will he serve as the tough punk rock singer, as the child who disrupted a whole world; rather he will now take himself as he is and ensure that what he is will be enough.

He will succeed. He will always succeed. He is now much too big for his image to fade; in retirement his legend will outlive him. A great natural artist, a monumental American figure, he now exists beyond mere talent or charisma.

The old Elvis is dead. The new one lives on. Hallelujah.

156

Afterword

The final words to the first edition of this book now hold a terrible irony: "The old Elvis is dead. The new one lives on. Hallelujah." Those words were written at the tail-end of 1974, when Elvis was performing in concert, at Las Vegas and on tour, to massive and often hysterically enthusiastic audiences. However, on 16 August 1977, Elvis, aged forty-two, after three years of illness, paranoia, indifferent performances and critical abuse, died of a heart attack in the bathroom of his home in Graceland, Elvis Presley Boulevard, Memphis, Tennessee.

His death was followed by nationwide mourning, scenes of mass hysteria, and a flood of media coverage of the kind that had not been seen since the death of President Kennedy. Newspapers gave the event the sort of coverage normally reserved for leading statesmen, and President Jimmy Carter, in an unprecedented gesture regarding a pop star, made a public statement, saying: "Elvis Presley's death deprives our country of a part of itself. His music and his personality, fusing the styles of white country and black rhythm and blues, permanently changed the face of American popular culture. His following was immense, and he was a symbol to the people the world over of the vitality, rebelliousness and good humour of this country." Similar tributes poured into Graceland from all corners of the globe, most notably from fellow performers of different generations, including Bing Crosby, Sammy Davis Jr, Elton John and numerous rock groups.

Elvis had been rushed on the night of the 16th to the Memphis Baptist Hospital, and the casket bearing his body arrived back in Graceland after noon the following day. Memphis mayor Wyeth Chandler declared a day of mourning for the city's 800,000 residents, and all flags on public buildings were at half mast. Florists were inundated with requests from all over the world, radio stations everywhere constantly played Elvis records, and traffic on the dual-carriageway Elvis Presley Boulevard (Route 51) was solid throughout the night. That same evening every one of the city's 9,000 hotel rooms was fully booked, and the local chamber of commerce had to make emergency arrangements to accommodate mourners in schools and homes. Meanwhile, Elvis's private DC9 jet was sent on a special mission to pick up his divorced wife Priscilla and Lisa, his adored nine-year-old daughter, at their home in Los Angeles. When Priscilla and Lisa arrived at the mansion that evening, the last love of Elvis's life, twenty-year-old model Ginger Alden, who bore a striking resemblance to Priscilla, was already inside being sedated. Elvis's father, sixty-one, and his grandmother, eighty-two, both with heart conditions, were also inside and under sedation.

Outside the mansion, thousands of fans had gathered in mourning. In scenes unparalleled since the death of Valentino, over a thousand security men and police fought to hold back the growing crowds as they attempted to break through the gates and scale the walls of Graceland. There were ten ambulances at the mansion, and inside the gates an emergency medical centre had been set up to treat the 300 people who had so far fainted. One woman had gone into labour pains and given birth in an ambulance.

To add horror to the tragedy, two teenage girls who had flown over a thousand miles to catch a final glimpse of their idol were killed when a car containing a black youth and three women drove deliberately at 60 mph into the crowd of mourners, hit a group of women, tried to run down the police at the gates, and was finally stopped when attempting to escape along Elvis Presley Boulevard. The two girls were killed instantly, another girl was critically injured, and the eighteen-year-old driver was charged with second degree murder, drunken driving and leaving the scene of an accident.

By 17 August, when Elvis was "lying in state" in the music-room of Graceland, 80,000 people had poured into Memphis from all over the world and were lining up along Elvis Presley Boulevard. The mansion was opened for two hours (later extended to three) to allow a large portion of the crowd to file past the casket and view the body. Elvis was dressed in a white cotton suit, blue shirt and white tie. His abdomen and legs were covered in red roses. On his right finger was a gold ring with a large red stone set in it. The casket itself was surrounded by red velvet drapes, and by numerous heavily-built, dark-suited men who, like Elvis, all had opulent rings on their fingers.

By 18 August, approximately 150,000 fans were lining the four-mile funeral route from Graceland to Forest Hills Cemetery, where Elvis's mother had also been buried. Said Sheriff David Barksdale: "I've been in law enforcement for twenty-seven years in Memphis and I've seen many events like the assassination of Martin Luther King – but I've never seen anything like this." That same day, while these fans were watching Elvis's funeral procession, sales of Elvis's newly-released album "Moody Blue" rocketed to 250,000, and shops the world over were selling out of every Elvis disc, book and poster in stock.

Only when Elvis's solid copper coffin had been slid into the mausoleum in Forest Hills Cemetery, on the afternoon of 18 August 1977, could many of the fans fully accept that The King was gone. The whole nation, and much of the world, was in an almost unprecedented state of shock.

A certain controversy surrounded the death. That Elvis should have died alone and unattended was a singularly brutal irony. Apparently he had been playing racket-ball with new love Ginger Alden in the grounds of Graceland that evening; before disappearing indoors, he waved to some fans outside the gates, who later reported that he had looked "really fit and very happy". Inside the mansion, Elvis had retired to the bathroom to read a book on religion and psychology – two subjects that had begun to obsess him in recent months. Ginger Alden went to sleep and awoke some hours later, at about 2.30 in the morning, to the realisation that Elvis was still in the bathroom. Disturbed, she opened the bathroom door.

"I thought at first he might have hit his head, because he had fallen out of his black lounging chair and his face was buried in the carpet. I slapped him a few times and it was like he breathed once when I turned his head. One of his eyes was just blood-red, and I couldn't move him." Racing from the bathroom, Ginger called for Elvis's road manager, Joe Esposito, who came running up the stairs. "When Joe turned Elvis's head over, I think he knew he was dead."

Elvis was rushed straight to the Memphis Baptist Hospital where, at approximately 3.30 that morning, the doctor said, "It's all over." It now seems that Elvis could have lain on the bathroom floor for about five hours, before being discovered by Ginger Alden.

First official reaction was from the Memphis police who announced that there was "a strong possibility" that Elvis had died from a drug overdose. A retraction was quickly issued and, after a preliminary examination of the body and subsequent autopsy, both Elvis's personal physician, Dr George Nichopoulos, and the Shelby County medical examiner, Dr Jerry Francisco, announced that Elvis had died of a cardiac arrhythmia, or abnormal heartbeat, due to undetermined causes. Beyond pointing out that Elvis had been receiving medical treatment for circulatory difficulties and excess weight, no further diagnosis was forthcoming. Both doctors also stated that there had been no evidence of excessive drug abuse – though the use of the word "excessive" leads one to suppose that there must have been evidence of *some* drug abuse.

However, while the doctors were denying evidence of drugs, ex-wife Priscilla was telling a very different story. "He was on speed (methadrine) and barbiturates," Priscilla said. "I almost destroyed my own life trying to get Elvis off his drug habit during our marriage." To add fuel to the fire (even before Elvis had been buried), journalist Chris Hutchins – who had known Elvis for thirteen years and had already cleaned up with a sensational exposé of the private pleasures of other pop stars – promptly rushed into print with some further information: "From my first meeting with him thirteen years ago – when he was already 'hooked' – I watched the pills, the capsules and the injections take their heavy toll of his health." Finally Red West, a bodyguard who had recently been fired by Elvis and had retaliated by co-authoring an exposé of his former mentor, jumped onto the bandwagon: "He was on pills all day long, and he would give himself shots in the arm and leg with little plastic syringes." And another aide confided to Chris Hutchins that Elvis had also been on a heavy cocaine kick.

It seems unlikely that Elvis died from an overdose (though cocaine has been mentioned, he was mostly on uppers and downers), but the drugs could certainly have contributed to the heart attack. From the evidence, it now seems clear that if Elvis wasn't on hard drugs, he was certainly taking vast amounts of pills in order to combat his fatigue, increasing depressions and general boredom.

Even before the October 1973 divorce from his wife, it had become obvious that Elvis was no longer happy. Stories of severe depressions and violent black rages began to emanate from Graceland; and combined with tales of his compulsive, almost neurotic overeating (hamburgers, Spanish omelets, ice-cream, fried banana and peanut butter sandwiches) were the more open signs of his degenerating health. He had started to put on weight, he often forgot the lyrics to songs, and he was in

and out of the Memphis Baptist Hospital with disturbing regularity. In 1973 he was admitted for "hypertension". Later that same year, he was readmitted for "intestinal blockage due to a twisting of the lower colon". Later still, he was readmitted for "gastric flu and fatigue". By 1977, after quite a few more spells in hospital, the diagnosis had progressed to "hypoglycaemia", a deficiency of sugar in the blood.

Since his hospitalisations were shrouded in secrecy, his numerous public performances were more revealing. For the first time in his two decades in show business, Elvis began cancelling shows, frequently talked more than he sang, read song lyrics from "idiot" boards, often sat in a chair due to his inability to continue standing, and even collapsed once or twice when on stage. Said the publicity director of the Baltimore Theatre of Elvis's April 1977 appearance there: "It was a shambles – a fiasco. He was so ill I didn't even think he knew where he was." Reviewing the same show, *Rolling Stone* magazine reported that Elvis performed for a mere twenty minutes, "at one point interrupting a request number by saying, 'Gimme the lyrics to this damn thing' ", after which he stumbled off stage, disappeared for half an hour, and eventually returned to finish his performance in a desultory fashion.

Common to these performances was Elvis's growing need to *talk* to the audience rather than sing to them. This talking took the form of long, rambling, brutally self-mocking speeches, during which he would compulsively emphasise that his health was fine and that he neither approved of, nor partook of, drugs. So obsessed was he with putting over this message that many fans soon became convinced (as did much of the media) that Elvis was definitely in ill health and on drugs.

Elvis first went into seclusion shortly after his mother's death. He did not truly emerge from the seclusion for another eight years, when he had married Priscilla and became the father of a daughter, Lisa. Adoring his new daughter, he seemed refired with enthusiasm and emerged from hiding to mount his brilliantly successful revival. From 1968 to mid-1973, he performed with great vitality and good humour. Then, when Priscilla left him, taking Lisa with her, Elvis started changing dramatically. Seemingly in a state of shock, unable to comprehend his loss, he continued to perform, but with desperation rather than enthusiasm, and once more he started hiding out in Graceland. It was from this point on that he embarked on self-parody, that his recording sessions became haphazard, and that stories started circulating about his compulsive overeating, his dependence on drugs, his fears of assassination, his belief that Graceland was haunted by his dead mother, his general dissatisfaction with Colonel Parker and the "Memphis Mafia" and with the glass-bowl existence he had been forced to endure.

Said pop star and personal friend Pat Boone: "He had a premonition that he would never live to be an old man because his mother had died fairly young, and that had a traumatic effect on him. . . . He was not in the best of shape lately, and he was very insecure. He told me he did not want to make another movie, and he seemed to dread his public appearances."

Elvis's physical and mental deterioration was brutally quick. Once the living embodiment of virility and sexuality, his weight suddenly shot up to a gross seventeen stone and he retreated into self-destructive hedonism. Contributing to this was the pain of being separated from his wife and beloved daughter, the humiliation of being constantly lambasted by both critics and fans, the knowledge that he was trapped by the enormity of his own fame (since the age of twenty he had not been able to walk out in public), and his shock over what he felt was a betrayal by some very old friends. In 1976 Elvis had finally fired various members of his entourage – the "Memphis Mafia" – including Sonny West, Red West and Dave Hebler. These three retaliated by co-operating on a ghost-written book that revealed the "inside story" of Elvis's carefully guarded private life.

Written in a sub-Spillane, sensationalist prose, the book told of Elvis's dependence on drugs, his terrifying rages, his increasingly desperate need to reaffirm his sexuality with a succession of younger and younger girls (videotaping his own love-making, and having mirrors installed in the ceiling of his bedroom), his fascination with guns and police work, and his equal fascination with death and the possibility of contacting his dead mother. All in all, what *did* come through the tawdry prose of the book was a picture of a desperately lonely man, dreading the approach of middle age, and trying to escape in drugs and childish hedonism. Elvis was shown a copy of the book just a few days before his death, and his doctor reported that he was "deeply shocked" by it. Whether or not it heightened his despair, and thus hastened his death, is a question that is written on the wind.

Given the failure of his personal life, his increasing failure as a public performer, and his growing feeling that he had lost touch with the real world, it is possible that Elvis willed himself into an early grave. Certainly more than one of his aides had stated that Elvis had recently seemed hell-bent on destroying himself.

Earlier in this book I wrote: "There is a sweet old cliché called the Trap of Success, and it is possible that even Elvis can't escape it. A consummate artist, he is cornered by his own image, by the breadth of his audience, by the size of his fame, by the mystique of his own presence, by financial considerations, by his age, and by the cold fact that most rockers lose their dignity in the end." Perhaps that's what happened. Perhaps he saw no hopeful future. Losing the fight against excess weight, turning defensively to self-parody, seeing himself as a future buffoon, the Mario Lanza of rock music, it is possible that he felt it wasn't worth it and thus wanted to escape.

In a remarkable essay on Marlon Brando (Brando's career has striking similarities to Elvis's) Pauline Kael put it in a nutshell: "It used to be said that great clowns, like Chaplin, always wanted to play Hamlet, but what happens in this country is that our Hamlets, like John Barrymore, turn into buffoons, shamelessly, pathetically mocking their public reputations." It is one of the more trenchant observations about American culture, and it applies with harrowing accuracy to Elvis Presley. Both Elvis and Marlon Brando represented what Kael called "a contemporary version of the free American" (both were primitive, physical and intuitive; both of them represented rebellion), and the similarities between them become even more apparent in the light of the fact that both endured approximately eight years of trashy work at approximately the same time – one, Brando, to return with a vengeance, and the other, Elvis, to return with equal success before surrendering once more to indifference.

Kael continues: "When you're larger than life you just can't be brought down to normalcy. It's easier to get acceptance by caricaturing your previous attitudes and aspirations, by doing what the hostile audience has already been doing to you . . . it is clear that for screen artists, and perhaps not only for screen artists, youth is, relatively speaking, the short season; the long one is the degradation *after* success."

Kael's essay on Brando was one of her finest hours, and it's application to Elvis is quite valid. Elvis was "larger than life", he was America's eternal "youth", and he paid the full price of the American Dream by finishing it in a particularly American way. Like John Barrymore, like Marilyn Monroe, like Orson Welles (still alive but ever parodying his earlier success), and, yes, like Howard Hughes, Elvis lived in the glass-bowl of unprecedented success and surrendered to self-mockery and then despair.

In the end, Elvis had given so much that there was nothing left to give. The creator of classic rock records, a ballad singer without peer, the leader of a revolution that he never comprehended, a stage performer of almost legendary charisma – in the end, the talent itself became superfluous. Certainly, during his final years, Elvis had merely to walk on stage and the applause was his before he started. Not for nothing would one of his most common onstage remarks be – when simply hitching up his belt or grinning that irresistible, immortal, lop-sided grin to incite hysterical enthusiasm in the audience – a remark usually spoken as a self-mocking aside to the band: "Hell, man, if *that's* all I gotta do I've got it made!" Well, in the end that's all he had to do. And Elvis knew it. And possibly couldn't live with it. And so, having no faith in his own artistic talent, having no way to expand it, isolated by his friends and sycophants and bodyguards, finding nothing in his art to support him, he turned his back on it all and searched out the peace that death had given to the mother who had protected him. Motherless, disenchanted, in a very real sense childless, Elvis Presley, a very great American artist, drove himself to the grave.

In the afternoon of 18 August 1977, after the mausoleum in Forest Hills Cemetery had been cleared of mourners, a group of workmen entered the crypt with a wheelbarrow full of sand, a bucket of water, cement and a box of tools. Working in silence they covered the crypt with a double slab of concrete and a final wall of marble, sealing the body of Elvis Presley in forever.

What has been left, and what will endure, is a testimony in song to the suffering, nobility and good humour of the human spirit. From gospel to rock, from the blues to simple ballads; from the exuberant "That's All Right (Mama)" to the orgasmic "Burning Love", from the hymnal "Can't Help Falling in Love" to the impassioned "Unchained Melody"; from the good to the bad, from the banal to the majestic – for over twenty years his music has encapsulated a growing culture and summed up the contradictions of artistic endeavour in a world where art and commerce must meet. A career of monumental heights and the most abysmal depths. An unparalleled success and a life lost before it was lived. Such figures become the mortar of History – and Elvis Presley is now History.

Acknowledgements

Anyone tackling an "illustrated biography" of Elvis Presley is bound to run into some headaches. Most of the classic early pictures of Elvis are no longer available from the press agencies, the fans who now hold them are understandably reluctant to part with them, and Presley's management refuses to cooperate "as a matter of policy" in "any literary endeavour". Which makes it a difficult field.

The majority of photographs in this book are the property of the Elvis Presley Appreciation Society which has over the years, with the assistance of its members, built up a considerable collection. I would therefore like to thank all the unknown fans who contributed this goldmine to the Appreciation Society, and the Society for letting me borrow it.

Special thanks must be offered to those individual fans who were willing to trust me with their memorabilia. These include my good friend Pøul Madsen, who sent me an enormous amount of material from Denmark; Penny Sayer, who poured the wine while I went through her remarkable trunk; the lovely Audrey Gussin, who also discussed Elvis at some length over a meal in the Golf Club; and Chris Handy, Melvyn Sergeant, Alan Beresford and Miss S. Whitfield, all of whom sent me material through the Fan Club. Thanks, also, to Lon Goddard of *Disc* for the use of his files; and to Jim Ellis for his general advice and assistance.

Most of the photographs of Elvis at Las Vegas and on tour are from the Metro-Goldwyn-Mayer films *Elvis: That's The Way It is* and *Elvis on Tour* and are courtesy of that company. Others are courtesy of Rex Features (photographs by Andy Sackheim), Camera Press (photographs by Terry O'Neil), Pictorial Press Ltd., Popperfoto (Paul Popper Ltd), United Press International (UK) Ltd., RCA Records, MGM-EMI Distributors, Paramount Films, Cinema International Corporation, 20th Century-Fox, United Artists, Allied Artists, National General Corporation, National Broadcasting Corporation, and photographers Sean Shavers, Uffe Lomholt Madsen and David Parkinson.

Thanks are due to the undermentioned copyright owners for permission to quote from the following songs:
Heartbreak Hotel reproduced by permission of Multimood Music Ltd., 230 Purley Way, Croydon, Surrey. *American Trilogy*, words by Mickey Newbury, reproduced by permission of Acuff Rose Music Ltd. *Tomorrow is a Long Time* reproduced by permission of Warner Bros. Music Ltd. *American Pie* reproduced by permission of United Artists Music Limited. *Suspicious Minds* reproduced by permission of Press Music. *Trouble* and *I'm Leavin'* reproduced by permission of Carlin Music Corporation, 17 Savile Row, London W1. *Bridge Over Troubled Water*, Copyright 1969, 1970 by Paul Simon. Permission to reproduce lyric granted by Pattern Music Ltd., 5 Denmark Street, London WC2.

With few exceptions, the "live" performances described in this book are not of any specific shows, but are compilations of various shows based on fan reports, reviews, newsreel and television footage, the two above named documentary films, and the author's own first-hand observations. However, special mention must be made of Louise O. Spencer of Virginia USA, and Ian Bailye of Leicester for their excellent reports, published in *Elvis* and *Elvis Monthly*, of Elvis performing in the mid-fifties.

Special note must also be accorded the following books, which gave me additional aid in the writing: *The Great American Popular Singers* by Henry Pleasants; *Elvis* by Jerry Hopkins; *Operation Elvis* by Alan Levy; *The Sound of the City* by Charlie Gillett; *Revolt Into Style* by George Melly; *Pop From The Beginning (Awopbopaloobop)* by Nik Cohn; *After the Ball* by Ian Whitcomb; *The Age of Rock* by Jonathan Eisen; and *The Sun Rock Session File* (Vol. 3) by Martin Hawkins and Colin Escott. The most valuable magazine articles were "A Far Cry From Home" by Pete Fowler and "Black Roots" by Clive Anderson, both to be found in the special "Elvis" issue of *Let It Rock*, December 1973. I was also indebted to David Dalton for his excellent report, *Elvis Presley: Wagging His Tail in Las Vegas*, originally published in *Rolling Stone* and currently included in *The Rolling Stone Rock 'n' Roll Reader*, edited by Ben Fong-Torres.

A very personal thanks to Tony Atkinson, Todd Slaughter, Vikki Slaughter and Manya Starr. Thanks also to all those who made my trip to Las Vegas so enjoyable: David Wade, Keith Harris, David Balson (for his protection), Marco van der Meij, Mark Wesley and Pierrette, Bill Conroy (say no more), Pøul Madsen (again) and of course the unforgettable Kirsten Ede.

Finally, thanks to Steve Ridgeway for designing the book, Julie Harris for assisting him, and Tony Power for his monumental patience during the final two weeks.

Allen Harbinson
June, 1975